"I'M ALL W...
THIS COULDN'T HAV...

In the beginning, many survivors go through a period of vacillating about the truth, feeling uncertain about whether they can trust their perceptions of reality. Many of the following are symptoms of other experiences. But if you have encountered any of them it may be a clue that you are an incest survivor:

- Do you have amnesia or memory loss for any periods of your childhood?
- Do you have intrusive memories or flashbacks of incidences that are traumatic to you?
- Are either of your parents alcoholic or addicted to drugs?
- Have you had trouble staying clean and sober in Twelve Step programs?
- Do you have a distasteful feeling about sex or your own sexuality?
- Do you choose abusive partners to be in relationship with?
- Do you have fears about getting too "closed in"?

REMEMBERING AND CLARIFYING MEMORIES CAN BEGIN THE RECOVERY PROCESS ...

RECLAIMING THE HEART

MARY BETH McCLURE, M.S., M.F.C.C.I., is a psychotherapist who has treated more than one hundred incest survivors. She specializes in chemical dependency, adult children
of alcoholics, and sexual abuse survivors. Mary Beth teaches
classes on the Twelve Steps for Recovery to therapists and
psychology students, and also conducts workshops on meditation and creative visualization.

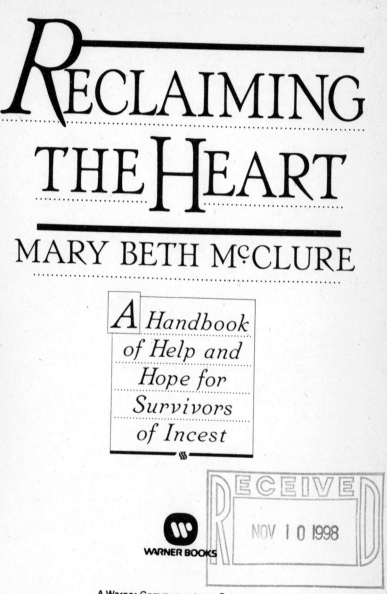

RECLAIMING THE HEART

MARY BETH McCLURE

A Handbook of Help and Hope for Survivors of Incest

§

WARNER BOOKS

A Warner Communications Company

The author gratefully acknowledges permission to quote from:

"Disturbances of Perception in Adult Female Incest Survivors" by Gerald Ellenson. *Social Casework*, March 1986. Published by Family Service America, Milwaukee, WI.

"Post Traumatic Stress Disorders in Women Who Experienced Childhood Incest" by F. Lindberg and Lois Distad. *Child Abuse and Neglect*, Vol. 9, 1985, Journal No. 586. Pergamon Press, Oxford, England.

"Treating Adult Survivors of Incest" by Geraldine Faria and Nancy Belonlavek. *Social Casework*, October 1984. Published by Family Service America, Milwaukee, WI.

Triumph over Darkness by Wendy Wood and Leslie Hatton. Beyond Words Publishing Co., Hillsboro, OR.

Warner Books, Inc., 666 Fifth Avenue, New York, NY 10103

A Warner Communications Company

Printed in the United States of America
First printing: July 1990
10 9 8 7 6 5 4 3 2 1

Library of Congress Cataloging-in-Publication Data

McClure, Mary Beth.
  Reclaiming the heart : a program for recovery from childhood sexual abuse and emotional incest / by Mary Beth McClure.
    p. cm.
  ISBN 0-446-39141-7
  1. Child molesting—United States. 2. Adult child abuse victims--United States. 3. Incest victims—United States. I. Title.
HQ72.U53M36   1990
362.7'6—dc20   89-70547
                                                        CIP

Designed by Giorgetta Bell McRee

Cover design by Louise Fili

Acknowledgments

I would like to acknowledge the generous support of the five women whose honesty and courage in telling their stories made this book possible.

I also offer my thanks to Mom, for teaching me about perseverance and a triumphant spirit, and to Dad, for your patience and strength and stability.

For emotional support when I was exhausted and for sharing the vision and joy, thank you to my incredible friends: Selwyn, Beth, Roland, Anne, Marta, Kelly, Laurel, Ashely, Liz, Nancy, Joyce, Genny, Nanette, Jimmy, Algera, Tom, Michelle, Chris, Judy, Maureen, Edie, and my sisters, K.T. and Sarah.

Thank you to Candice Fuhrman and Leslie Keenan for bringing this dream to a reality, to Peter Beren and Dr. Julie Lewis, Dr. Robert Suczek, and Dr. Steele, and many, many thanks to Barbara Brauer of Wordsworth Inc. for your precision and skill and your gentle style.

To everyone in the struggle and joy of recovery
and
to Pat—for teaching me about opening my heart
through your constant example of love.

Contents

CONTENTS

Author Note:
Why I Work in This Field

My mother was molested by her alcoholic father for many years, beginning when she was two until she was about seventeen. Miraculously, unlike so many others she did not marry an offender and thus perpetuate this cycle of abuse, carrying it to another generation. Instead her incest memories went "underground" and were completely repressed. The repressed memories did, however, have a powerful and pervasive effect on her life and on the new family she tried to create. This effect permeated all of her family relationships, marital and parent-child.

In her superhuman attempt to be a perfect wife and mother, my mom tried to make certain that everything looked okay on the outside. This "looking good" was actually an attempt to manage her anxiety. My mother stood on guard constantly to keep her childhood memories of abuse at bay. This guarding took many forms: obsessive-compulsive concerns about cleanliness, disease, and germs, and various terrors about her children's safety. The terror manifested itself in a kind of hypervigilance about possible danger—fears that we'd fall if we were too active, fears of passing trucks on roads, of elevators, tunnels, and more.

Her repression of the abuse memories also produced a tendency to unpredictably "fade away" or "check out" emotionally, because, unknown to any of us, she had been exposed to a memory trigger and was fighting extra-hard to keep the recall from occurring. All I knew was that "nobody was home," that sometimes my mom was far away and I couldn't figure out what I had done wrong to make her go away.

What I know today is that a parent with a gaping emotional wound, a raw sore, an empty hole at her core cannot attend to the needs of her children. The child's cues signaling needs for closeness and for separation will be misread or not responded to at all, because the parent is so busy, internally, trying to manage her own unmet needs. The child will grow up feeling alone, lost, and vaguely or blatantly at fault for a level of pain whose source is never seen.

My mother's inner world was filled with terror. The "bogeyman under the bed" that haunts every child had been a reality for her—a living nightmare from which there was no comfort. My mother's ability to bond with me and then allow me to separate from her was damaged; she alternated between periods of extreme neediness and fearfulness, on the one hand, and depressive withdrawals, on the other. Having no imprinting of what real family relationships could be like, my mother constructed a caricature-like fantasy version, taken from television images and her imagination. These models posed very high ideals and, when expected life crises confronted the family, there were no problem-solving tools available. The family took on my mother's coping skills of repression and denial, and simply pretended the problems didn't exist—not the most efficient way to create solutions. Because we followed the unspoken edicts to "look good" and "be normal" at all costs, anger was not allowed to be expressed in our family. My sisters and

I got very good at being "good girls"—at least until adolescence.

It is not uncommon for children to act out the unspoken, unconscious, and unresolved issues of their parents, particularly during puberty. This is a time when a family's "skeletons in the closet" come to life. The adolescent lives out a drama she didn't even know existed, its authors being several generations buried.

Because unspoken messages jump generations in families if kept secret, I sensed my mother had not been adequately cared for. I attempted to become a care-giver to my mother as she, in a more extreme way, had been a care-giver to her father. As indicated by this childhood sense of responsibility to take care of my mother, there were no clear boundaries in my family. A family with this kind of undifferentiated pain cannot create generational boundaries, in terms of which parents are parents and kids are allowed to be kids without the burden of adult roles. I arrived at puberty without a strong sense of self and full of ambivalence about separating from my mother. Although I had been an "A" student and a good athlete and everything looked good on the outside, I was riddled with questions about my self-worth and terrified of men.

My mother could not commuicate to me that a womanly body is lovable, that the world is a good and safe place, or that men are not here to hurt women. As they say in Alcoholics Anonymous (a self-help program that deals with similar issues—alcoholism is also generationally transmitted), "You can't transmit what you don't have." Instead of being able to affirm my image of myself as a woman, verbally and nonverbally, my mother's painful and negative feelings about her body, her shame about her gender, and her fear of men were transferred to me. In the thousands of ways parents transmit to their children their innermost thoughts and beliefs—through attitudes, silences, tones of voice, facial expressions, grimaces, eye contact, touch (or lack thereof)—she communicated to me the experience for which she had no language.

My chemical dependency surfaced when I was twelve, just when my sexuality was emerging. Tequila and Quaaludes were my drugs of choice. Using alcohol and barbiturates provided a perfect temporary solution to my conflicts by allowing me to anesthetize the feelings of loneliness, confusion, and guilt that haunted me. My acting-out behavior made me feel like a rebel while I obediently followed my mother's unspoken injunction: "Take care of me/Don't leave me." Because I was too busy getting drunk to learn any self-care skills, I didn't really master the developmental tasks of adolescence. My emotional maturity was arrested at twelve, the age I started drinking. My difficulty with setting personal boundaries carried over to my relationships with peers and men, and was exaggerated when I was under the influence. Not being able to say no to men caused me to put myself in abusive situations, thereby repeating a version of the sexual abuse cycle for one more generation.

In the fascinating way that families develop symptoms in an attempt to heal themselves, my staggering gait and the smell of alcohol on my breath triggered the release of my mother's incest memories that had by now been hidden away for more than twenty years. Six years later we both entered recovery: My mother got into therapy and I got sober through self-help support groups. The changes in our lives and in the entire family structure are nothing short of miraculous.

After fourteen years of recovery in Twelve Step programs (and many years of therapy and professional training), I have come to work as a psychotherapist, specializing in chemical dependency and work with adult children of alcoholics. It was during this work that I stumbled back into the issues of childhood sexual abuse and emotional incest. I discovered a group of clients who seemed incapable of trusting; they carried the same tendency to "split off" from contact that I had experienced with my mother. This "splitting off" or "numbing out" interfered with every level of relationship in these clients' lives: from social and professional issues to, more painfully, attempts to be sexual and to relate to their children.

I began to identify a cluster of symptoms that was a string of clues screaming loudly for recognition: self-mutilation, destructive relationships, sexual acting-out or asexual feelings, and eating disorders. Another more quietly painful symptom of childhood sexual abuse is what I call the "invisible person" syndrome—the learned tendency to make oneself unnoticeable in the presence of others. This is accomplished by body posturing (head held down, a slight "cringing" in the shoulders and neck); lack of eye contact or a glazed look over the eyes; a low, flat tone of voice; and/or a choice of drab color and style of clothes. With some clients, there seemed to be an inability to form a bond or therapeutic alliance with me or even believe that I would be there for them from one week to the next. The shame went so deep and the belief in the efficacy of human bonds was so tentative that these women's substance abuse recovery was fragile and their relapse potential was very high.

I began to develop a personal commitment to working with survivors and consider it a great privilege. I've watched these clients running from their "shadows in the night," from the ghosts that endlessly haunt them, in their most private lives and intimate moments. I've listened as the vague memories become fuller and stronger—as the uncertainty becomes clearer and brighter and the deep recognition dawns that, "Yes, something did happen to me as a child." I've witnessed the loss and grief hit the surface and the full force of pain and rage become unleashed. Gradually, this flooding phase subsides and gives way to a deepening acceptance and a quiet dignity that comes from knowing one has survived. The feeling at this point is something like: "I lost a part of me that I don't know if I can ever reclaim. My innocence—my child's blind trust that my caretakers won't hurt me—is gone. But I can learn to take care of that child in myself now. I can make choices and reparent my Inner Child and reclaim my heart." I've watched these women choose to open their hearts and get the scattered, split-off pieces of themselves back, slowly reclaiming the childhood that was stolen from them.

The survivors in my life have been some of my most powerful spiritual teachers. They continue to show me that it is possible to rebuild a self, in spite of sustained injury, and to reclaim the heart. I believe survivors of sexual abuse are the unsung heroes of our time. These women have waited in silence and shame for their story to be told. It is time we listened.

Introduction

Millions of people have been sexually abused as children. As the subject of incest is more openly discussed, many women are beginning to wonder if they, too, are survivors of childhood abuse.

If this is something you are wondering about, this book can guide you through the process. Recovery from sexual abuse and emotional incest is possible. It has predictable phases. This book will guide you step by step through those phases, showing you a way to understand both your present experience and what you might expect in the future. It will help you to recognize the long-term residual effects of sexual abuse, and the feelings and behavior you may confront as you travel through recovery. You will learn how to use various treatment and recovery tools in this process.

The first step to incest recovery is breaking denial. Incest cannot exist without denial. As a society, we are only now starting to come out of denial about the prevalence, severity, and variety of the several forms of incest. This is why more facts and information are coming out, and why more survivors are now willing to tell their stories. But there is still a powerful taboo in our society that reinforces denial. Society's refusal to acknowledge the widespread presence of childhood sexual abuse and the low incidence of reporting make obtaining accurate statistics difficult. Until recently few statistics were available except from studies done on incarcerated offenders.

The facts beginning to be reported are:

One out of four girls will be sexually assaulted before she turns eighteen, a statistic reported by Parents United, a national self-help group for incest survivors and their families.

One in every six stepdaughters will be an incest victim, according to Diana Russell, researcher and author of *The Secret Trauma*.

Even therapists and others in the helping professions have often misdiagnosed survivors. We are only now beginning to see symptoms that were formerly given psychiatric labels (such as "multiple personality disorder" and sometimes "borderline" and "hysterical personality" syndromes) recognized in many cases as the residual effects of incest and other kinds of trauma (Courtois, 1988, pp. 148–62).

The present response to sexual abuse can be likened to people's reluctance to respond to chemical dependency (alcoholism and drug addiction) ten to twenty years ago, before the sheer number of recovering people helped to shift the stigma of that "secret disease." For example, few researchers have explored the short- and long-term consequences of incest, the symptoms of which may include sexual dysfunction, promiscuity, running away, prostitution, adolescent pregnancy, depression, intense guilt, drug or alcohol abuse, anxiety, somatic complaints, learning difficulties, and marital problems.

In fact, chemical dependency and incest survivor issues are closely linked in two ways:

There is a greater chance of sexual abuse in alcoholic homes. (Fifty percent of incest victims are from alcoholic homes [Black, 1981].)

Survivors of sexual abuse fequently become addicted. (Up to 80 percent of chemically dependent women are estimated to be incest survivors [National Abortion Rights Action League, n.d.].)

Like alcoholism, sexual abuse is an intergenerational disease: Incest survivors often marry molesters, who then abuse their children. Molested children (especially boys) abuse other children, particularly younger siblings. Deprived, confused children grow up to become parents, only to re-create the cycle of abuse and despair one more time, unless they receive treatment. This cycle can be stopped only through education—of survivors, their families and friends, educators and therapists, and the public at large—about the signs and symptoms of sexual abuse and emotional incest, so that earlier detection and treatment can occur.

Sexual abuse survivors today are on the cutting edge of changing future generations by recovering, first from within, and then by bringing that recovery to the rest of society.

WHAT IS RECOVERY?

Through my work counseling adult survivors I've observed some common patterns that seem to forge a blueprint for recovery.

Recovery is an intricate process of identifying, acknowledging, and healing the wounds left by sexual abuse and emotional incest. The phases defined here are not definitive, nor are they necessarily sequential. Incest survivor recovery, like other recovery, is a process that is more circular than linear. It can be likened to a series of cycles that treat and resolve certain issues common among the recovery population, although each journey is unique.

These issues usually include:

1. Identifying yourself as a survivor of emotional (or covert) incest or sexual abuse. When making this identification, it is important to define whether you have any memory loss (amnesia) about any periods of your childhood and to detect symptoms of Post-traumatic Stress Disorder syndrome.

2. Locating resources and support systems that will be essential to you in recovery.

3. Preparing yourself to successfully deal with essential issues by becoming clean and sober—or free from other obsessive-compulsive urges—so that your real feelings can begin to surface, thus clearing the way for the recovery process to begin. Obsessive-compulsive urges are those behaviors that you feel driven to do by repetitive, intrusive thoughts.

4. Beginning to identify and feel your feelings. It is usually necessary to reexperience both grief and anger, to learn how to identify boundaries and develop a sense of self. Having a true self means knowing what you need, want, and feel, and allowing yourself to see what you see and know what you know, rather than denying your reality when it doesn't agree with the reality of others. It means having a connection to your body, your sexuality, and your sensations.

5. Reaching the wounded child within, learning how to play and how to trust your inner voice or intuition. Having an energized core self comes from "reparenting" yourself and discovering a state of self-love. This is the basis for allowing love into your life and developing the capacity for intimacy.

6. Developing the ability to care for yourself, to have dreams and visions for your future, to problem-solve rather than avoid problems, and to make choices rather than simply react. You should be free to go forward to live your life as an adult without carrying the baggage of events that occurred in the past. You may find ways to express the suffering, recasting it into forms that speak to others. The final phase of recovery is signaled by a new sense of energy, meaning, and purpose for your life and the absence of remorse and shame.

One of the highest costs of sexual abuse is to live in a world without color or hope and never know there is another way. By some miraculous resiliency of the human spirit, it is possible to break the chains forged by this seemingly incomprehensible abuse and move beyond basic survival issues into a richness that you may have never even known was missing from your life.

This book is for you, the survivor. It describes the contours of the recovery process, the shift from the darkness of doubt and shame to the discovery of light and freedom. Too many women are hiding their sexual abuse under substance abuse, eating disorders, or physically or verbally abusive relationships. Or they are simply cut off from the fullness of life because they, like my mother, must complete a bewildering array of obsessive-compulsive rituals to try to feel safe. Emotional incest survivors are chronic caretakers and underachievers, the "lives of quiet desperation" that never move into a state of joy or actualization. This book is written for all survivors—but especially for the chemically dependent survivors who can't stay clean because the pain of life with memories of childhood abuse is too unbearable without drugs.

There are sections in the back of this book for therapists and people in the helping professions, and for partners of survivors.

Many people may ask if there is some danger for a survivor working alone with a book on this potentially volatile issue. *Reclaiming the Heart* is not intended to be a substitute for therapy or involvement in any one of the number of cost-free support groups listed in the following pages. It is important for an adult survivor to have other human beings actively involved in her recovery process. Much of the healing occurs in the telling of one's story to another person who understands. However, when a survivor is just learning to trust or can't yet put words to feelings, it is useful to read about how others survived and healed this wound.

Important: If at any time during your recovery work, thoughts and feelings of wanting to hurt yourself come up, the first step is to get to a safe place. If you need to get to a safe place, do it! Go to a crisis unit or talk to someone immediately. Most communities have an agency with a counselor available twenty-four hours a day; call them or a suicide hot line or self-help line. The objective is to provide containment. Call your therapist. Go see a friend; go to a Twelve Step meeting or clubhouse. As a last resort, get in bed. Do whatever it takes to slow down and not act on the impulse.

Then, when the feeling has passed, take a moment to try to recognize the first thought that set off the compulsion. If you can stop the process at the first thought, there will be less escalating, emotionally and physically, and less "wreckage" to deal with later. You don't have to act on a thought just because you have it. You can learn what to do to master it. For more information on obsessive-compulsive disorders, particularly chemical dependency, turn to Chapter Three.

SOME DEFINITIONS

For the purposes of this book, *sexual abuse* is considered to be a continuum of inappropriate behavior between a child and an adult family member. This behavior may range from direct sexual interactions to the more subtle forms of violating a child's boundaries through *emotional* and *covert incest.*

A *child* is anyone under the age of eighteen. An *adult* is anyone at least seven years older than the child, the age difference creating a power differential.

Sexual interactions include but are not limited to fondling, French kissing, fellatio, mutual masturbation, penetration, and intercourse.

Covert incest is defined as household voyeurism, ridicule of developing bodies, "inadvertent" touching, sexual hugs, the use of sexualizing language that reduces females to objects or body parts, and strong unconscious or latent sexual fantasy between a parent and child. *Emotional incest* is the violation of a child's boundaries by using the child to satisfy the unmet needs of the parent; it is the assigning of an adult role to a child. The effects of emotional incest are damage to the development of a sense of self and difficulty setting limits, particularly in relationships. The effects of covert incest are confusion, guilt, a sense of impending doom, and major distortions in the development of a sexual identity.

We are just beginning to recognize that the effects of covert incest, while more subtle, can be pervasive, devastating, and long-lasting. One way of understanding this is to see a continuum of developmental damage occurring from emotional incest, covert incest, and sexual abuse. The range is from the interruption of establishing a sense of self that occurs when a child experiences emotional incest from a pathologically needy parent; to disruption of sexuality in covert incest; to the increased violation and deep trauma of sexual abuse.

Survivors are women eighteen years old and older who experienced sexual abuse during childhood or adolescence. This book will deal only with women survivors.

My focus on women survivors is not intended to negate the occurrence of sexual abuse of males or the very real need for recovery information for men incest survivors. Many of the issues men survivors confront are similar to women's, but many are unique. If you are a male survivor, please take whatever you can use from this book.

HOW TO USE THIS BOOK

Reclaiming the Heart is designed to be used as a map, and a companion, for your journey through your own uncharted internal territory. For some readers, just opening this book may bring up feelings of fear, confusion, or shame. Remember, you are not alone; you are not crazy. Recovery is a path that many have walked before you.

You don't have to take this trip alone; there are others to guide you, offering their support every step of the way. And you don't have to do anything before you are ready. Reading this map does not commit you to anything. You can read it now just to learn more about the territory, in case you ever decide to travel through it. You can take this book part by part, exploring small sections at a time and returning regularly to your starting point. Or you can commit to a long journey, having made the decision that you will do whatever it takes to discover your own power and become a whole person.

Within each chapter you will find a variety of treatment and recovery tools and practical techniques I call "processes" that can assist you in your recovery. These processes are designed to work through the feelings that accompany each phase of recovery, from breaking denial and grieving, to expressing and releasing rage and arriving at resolution. The therapeutic tools offered are taken from my own experience in counseling sexual abuse survivors and from a survey of other therapists' work in this new and expanding field.

You can decide how fast and how far you want to go, how much you want to open up and how much you need to close down. With the map in your hand now, you are in charge of your own destiny and your own recovery.

It is important that you set the pace at which you approach this kind of information and experience, and the format of this book enables you to do that. Every survivor has her own source of wisdom and strength. See if you can trust your wisdom to guide you through this workbook, and to the people and situations that feel nurturing and healing to you. You don't have to read every chapter or do every exercise, or "process." If you are reading something that feels overwhelming, put the book down for a while. Or go back to a previous chapter and work through the processes in that chapter. Continue to work with a process until you feel ready to move forward again. If you're reading something that seems familiar, skip to the next chapter if you want, until you feel challenged. Follow what moves you. Something inside you knows what you need and how to heal; this book is simply an aid for you to get in touch with that part of yourself and connect with it in a deeper way.

It is a good idea to have a therapist or sponsor with whom to share your process work, particularly if you are working with your feelings. It is normal to go through periods of great grief and anger. If you don't have a therapist or support group, this book can help you find one.

Among the most valuable resources to people in recovery are the stories of others who have made the journey. Hearing what they experienced, how they felt, and what they found along the way is a great source of information and affirmation. For this reason, the stories of five recovering survivors have been included to illustrate different aspects of recovery and to give you a chance to hear them tell their own stories, in their own words. It is my hope that you will discover the power and the beauty within each one, and find the same in your own story. Through listening to their voices, you may find your own.

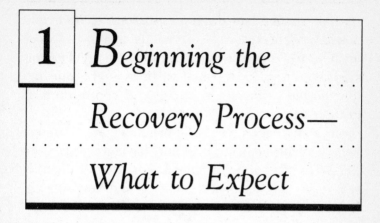

1 Beginning the Recovery Process— What to Expect

BREAKING DENIAL

Most women begin recovery with little or no certainty that they are survivors of sexual abuse and/or emotional incest. This is because most incest survivors experience either partial or full amnesia about the actual event. As a result they may vacillate between believing the incest occurred and thinking, "I'm all wrong. This couldn't have happened."

Sometimes, when the memories of the incest are crystal clear, their feelings about it are frozen. At other times, survivors experience "flooding feelings" or rushes of memories without any understanding of where the feelings originate. Some of these individuals see images or fragments of visual pictures. Others begin to have new reactions to certain sounds, smells, or tastes, to books or movies, as the numbing starts to thaw. Sometimes nameless fears arise and develop into specific phobias, such as feeling afraid to leave the house, drive a car, cross a bridge, be in a small space, or be touched in a certain area of the body. Fear or anger toward men or sexual partners might come up unexpectedly, along with a sense of confusion and disorientation.

For still others, there is simply a nagging, haunted feeling of never being safe and having to stay constantly in control or on guard. For these women, a real crisis may seem preferable to endlessly waiting for something terrible to happen or a lingering sense of impending doom. That is why survivors who begin to get close to their memories during therapy may find themselves doing self-destructive things, such as sabotaging the therapy or "going blank."

No matter which of these experiences, if any, you have had, your first task in recovery will be to determine the presence of any amnesia about your past, and to rediscover and/or clarify feelings and memories so that you can identify yourself as an incest survivor. It is common to bounce back and forth for a period of time, feeling uncertain about whether you can trust your perceptions of reality. Yet as you continue to gather information about incest recovery, bringing yourself in contact with the stories of survivors and other sources of information, this uncertainty will begin to lift. If the incest occurred, that will get clearer; if it didn't occur, that will get clearer, too.

POST-TRAUMATIC STRESS DISORDER

In recent years significant findings have been recorded about the long-term effects of trauma. These findings help to explain why incest memories are so frequently repressed and why certainty about the abuse is elusive. Many of these long-term symptoms of incest survival have been attributed to what researchers have termed Post-traumatic Stress Disorder (PTSD). Incest survivors, as well as adult children of alcoholics and Vietnam War veterans, have been found to exhibit such symptoms as "intrusive imagery of the incident, feelings of detachment or constricted affect (or numb, cut-off feelings), sleep disturbance, guilt, and intensification of symptoms when exposed to events resembling the trauma" (*Diagnostic Statistical Manual*).

Lindberg and Distad suggest that the reason adult clients seek help many years after the incest abuse is because "following a severe trauma, a pattern of repression, denial and emotional avoidance emerges. This denial-numbing phase, also called a latency period, can last days or decades, and then is followed by an intrusive repetitive phase."

Gelinas (1983) described the phenomenon in the following way:

> The first response to a traumatic event is usually outcry. When that doesn't work, denial sets in with periodic breakthrough memories of the trauma. This is called "phasic

denial with intrusions." This period is accompanied by a variety of nonspecific symptoms. It is not uncommon to have all thoughts about the trauma wiped out, and a numbing of feelings. Any thoughts or emotions that would remind the survivor of the trauma are also warded off.

Gelinas further notes:

Because incest tends to be a repetitive trauma, and the victim is repeatedly in some contact with the offender over a long period of years, total denial about the incest does not always occur. Instead survivors may deny the importance of the experience. They may also repress particularly disturbing elements or periods of time, initially reporting few memories of childhood, or of the incest experiences.

One common symptom survivors often exhibit is a tendency to disassociate or "leave their bodies" when under stress, even after the incest stops. In the midst of an experience, a person feels as through she is not quite joined to her body even while a part of her observes the experience and can describe it afterward. Disassociation often indicates a flashback of the traumatic experience. When the body and mind become overwhelmed with stimuli, they simply shut down and stop processing information until the system is no longer overloaded. This is perfectly natural. Everybody splits off from their experiences occasionally; we call it daydreaming. But for a survivor, rather than being a mildly pleasurable reprieve from discomfort, this splitting off is an unconscious necessity that interferes with her ability to "stay present." She is unable to participate in experiences whether she wants to or not, because a partial memory of a disturbing past event has been triggered.

EMOTIONAL INCEST

If you are an emotional or covert incest survivor, it may be especially difficult for you to recognize and acknowledge the fact that you have been abused. This kind of incest has a range of forms, from blatant to subtle, that can be very hard to pinpoint.

Emotional incest refers to the lack of *emotional boundaries* between a parent and a child. For example, it is emotional incest when a parent keeps a child an "emotional hostage" by using the child, mentally or emotionally, to meet the parent's own needs. When a child has a sense that her parent is constantly "hovering," and that she is responsible for her parents' emotional well-being, or when she is placed in the position of substitute spouse, preferred playmate, or confidante for marital problems—it is emotional incest.

Parents with healthy emotional boundaries should know where they end and their child begins and be willing to come to the task of parenting to give. A parent should take complete responsibility for his or her own life and sense of well-being before having a child, not expect a child to fill up or take care of him or her in any way. Children have natural nurturing and caring feelings for their parents and, of course, should feel free to express them. But it is not a child's job to parent a parent. A child's job is to be a child, which means to be highly needy, egocentric, and self-absorbed. Children learn to give this up in small doses over many years. The only way for a child to become less needy is to be given to. Children need to spend about the first five years of their lives simply absorbing into themselves the image and experience of a parent who loves them. This is called *internalizing* a "good mother" or "good father." This experience becomes the basis for a *sense of self* or a *core self* that has enough stamina to begin the process of separation or *individuation*. Individuation is the ability to experience oneself as a separate, unique, lovable, and capable human being who can move in and out of relationships with others successfully. So, through the experience of bonding and then being set free in graduated doses, a child develops the skills to operate skillfully in the world. Children need all their energy for their own developmental tasks; from mastering their senses and muscles to learning signaling behavior and language, to exploring the world—including socialization and relating to others with trust and a healthy sense of initiative and creativity—to becoming sexual beings and discovering a profession. Children who are burdened with emotional incest are going to miss their own developmental work. They will arrive at adulthood deficient in one of these areas or "developmentally arrested" at whatever age they had to give up their internal work to focus prematurely on an external task. If a parent needs parenting, a child will automatically and instinctively turn to that task, since making sure a wounded parent is okay is the only way to insure survival. Every child is hyper-alert to this, on a deep level.

No parent is perfect or expected to be a saint. Of course a parent can't be constantly giving without developing undue resentment of the child. But the decision to parent should be taken on as a job that requires an output of energy, commitment, and devotion. In order to do this, parents must refuel. They will need to refuel from sources other than children, preferably other adults.

A child who is raised with the expectation that he or she is responsible for a parent's feelings or emotional well-being is experiencing *enmeshed boundaries*. Frequently when there is an unresolved marital conflict (particularly one that is buried or secret), a child will be pulled in to fill the missing need. Being expected to take on a missing marital partner's role is an inappropriate job for a child. Kids should not be married. Marriage is for grown-ups. There should be a boundary between the adults and the children in a family. These are called *generational boundaries*, meaning there is a separation of emotional needs between one generation and the next. It is easy to see how a cycle of deprivation gets passed down from one generation to the next. If parents have children to fill an unconscious wish to get the love they never received from their own parents, they raise children who become adults but secretly feel angry and ripped off that they never had a childhood. They, in turn, expect inappropriate nurturing from their own kids, and the chain continues.

To present a balanced picture, it should be noted that we are only beginning to be able to track these kind of issues, with the advent of available birth control and a strong women's movement that truly give people the *choice* to become parents. However, children raised in enmeshed families or emotionally incestuous environments still need to take stock of their losses and begin the process of recovering a sense of true self and the capacity to have healthy relationships. The scars of a stolen childhood are a horrible, haunting sense of emptiness, even though everything may look fine in their family. Self-destructive behavior, an inability to set limits, and a feeling of not really existing, of not being quite real, this is the toll taken on emotional incest survivors. Other symptoms are:

fears of being trapped

panic attacks, claustrophobia

inability to tolerate closeness or commitment in relationships

being "commitment-phobic" in a variety of areas: jobs, geographic areas, sexual partners

chronic underachievement

chronic lateness

choosing destructive relationships; needy, demanding partners codependency

irritability or rage when asked to be dependable/ account for self

indecisiveness

impulsiveness

This syndrome is common in daughters of incest survivors and adult children or grandchildren of alcoholics where there was no further abuse, as well as survivors of covert incest and/or sexual abuse.

See Chapter Six, "Recovering Sexuality," for more information and Processes on "Discovering Your Boundaries."

COVERT INCEST

Another more "loaded" or potentially volatile form of incest is covert incest. This form of incest involves a parent's sexual desires more than their emotional needs. An example of covert incest is a parent using a child as a sexual fantasy object in a repetitious, inappropriate way or touching the child inappropriately. Note: This is to be distinguished from a parent having an occasional sexual fantasy or erotic, sensual reaction to a child, which is normal and expectable.

Other examples of covert incest include situations in which a child:

is voyeuristically stared/looked at

is ridiculed for her developing body or made to feel unsafe for her emerging sexuality

is spoken to or treated like a sexual object

is exposed to pornographic material for the purpose of arousing the adult

is expected to describe details of her sexual activity

has a strong, recurring "creepy feeling" about the way she is touched, looked at, or talked about by a parent

Some of the effects of covert incest are hyper-vigilance, a constant need to stay on guard for potential danger, never being able to really relax; having negative, "dirty," or frightened feelings about one's sexuality; and confusion about personal boundaries in relationships. In addition, covert incest survivors may experience:

negative body image

negative feelings about sex or fear of the power of her sexuality

feelings of guilt, shame, or that she must be constantly hiding something

a need to attempt to be "invisible" through the use of submissive body posturing and a style of dressing that draws attention away from the body

feelings of contempt, fear of and/or anger at men

difficulty with her sexual arousal responses: an inability to "let go"

difficulty maintaining interest in sex with a committed and/or interested partner or letting others get close

inability to have an orgasm or center her focus on her own sensations during sexual experiences

a sense of impending doom or forboding; never really feeling safe or grounded in her own body

If you are an emotional or covert incest survivor, it is very important for you not to discount your experiences, especially when you begin to hear the stories of women who have experienced overt sexual incest. If your ability to function as a free, autonomous, sexual, adult woman has been impaired, or if your functioning is anything less than the highest optimal level that it could have been without the abuse, you have reason to grieve and be angry and to claim your strengths as a survivor.

COMMON INDICATORS OF CHILDHOOD INCEST IN ADULT SURVIVORS

Because many symptoms typically associated with incest are similar to those seen in adult children of alcoholics (ACAs) who don't have a history of incest, you may want to read through the following list of twelve indicators that may indicate the occurrence of incest more directly. A few of these symptoms may also be common for ACAs, but having more than two or three symptoms, particularly numbers nine through twelve, is more indicative of sexual abuse.

1. *Amnesia.* Not the absence of recall, but rather gaps in the recall of periods of early childhood and adolescence. Amnesia may be an indicator that some kind of abuse occurred during this time. (See the sections "Amnesia" and "Processes to Work on Amnesia," below, for more information.)

2. *Phobias or anxiety attacks.* Events that may include claustrophobia, panic attacks, and a general sense of dread. The anxiety may be attached to a specific experience such as a fear of tunnels, bridges, tight places, high places, dark places, being alone, or being in the middle of a crowd. Symptoms may be converted into physical complaints that include head and neck pain, tingling, paralysis of the extremities, nausea, and gastrointestinal distress.

3. *Flashbacks, nightmares, or intrusive recollections that happen in both waking and sleeping states.*

4. *Negative differentness.* A feeling that one is diseased, bad, and dirty. The survivor may also imagine that others can observe this negative differentness just by looking at her.

5. *Isolation from peers.* Current or past tendencies not to want to associate with others, which can be masked by excessive activity or work or simply not leaving the house.

6. *Distorted perception of parenting figures.* Viewing

one's parents as idealized or omnipotent, possessing unrealistic powers, or, conversely, as fragile and weak, requiring special caretaking.

7. *Low self-esteem/massive guilt.* Feelings that may be demonstrated by self-mutilation or repeated involvement in abusive relationships.

8. *Depression.* Usually chronic, depression may range from low energy, agitation, and diminished interest in activities to estrangement from others.

9. *Body image concerns.* Preoccupations with one's physical presentation, which may be expressed by a particularly provocative and seductive appearance, or by being slovenly and self-neglecting. This category may also include obesity, anorexia, and uncontrolled eating disorders.

10. *Dissociative episodes or fugue states.* Out-of-body experiences that often occur during sexual activity or demands for intimacy. (See "Processes to Identify 'Splitting Off.'")

11. *Stimulus avoidance/startle response.* A feeling of being unusually jumpy or all "keyed up" in certain situations.

12. *Historical signposts*, such as a family history of:

Alcoholism in one or both parents

Physical or mental disability in one or both parents

Isolated family with few friends or social contacts

Chronic urinary tract and/or vaginal infections in childhood

Sudden drop in school performance or chronic underachievement

Early flight from home that may take the form of runaway behavior

Extensive psychiatric histories, including numerous therapists, conflicting diagnoses, frequent hospitalization, and drug therapy

History of prostitution, pornography, and related "promiscuous" behaviors

SPECIFIC INCEST SURVIVOR SYMPTOMS

The most specific diagnostic indicators of incest are those cited by Gerald Ellenson in "Disturbances of Perception in Adult Female Incest Survivors."

Ellenson discovered one symptom that seems to be unique to incest survivors, which he calls "visual and auditory hallucinations." However, he gives the word *hallucination* a different meaning than that typically employed by psychiatry. What Ellenson discovered is that survivors are disturbed by repetitive, intrusive sounds and images. These images or pictures have some common themes, which appear to be universal and unique to women who have been sexually abused. The images are of "shadowy figures, always described as dark, featureless silhouettes, nearly always experienced as male, evil, and/or dangerous." Sometimes the shadowy figure is moving; other times it is standing still. When the figure is immobile it is frequently reported to appear to survivors at the foot of their bed when they are lying in bed. The figure is miragelike; when a survivor stares hard, the image disappears.

The moving figure appears to survivors during the day and the night and is often in or around the survivor's home. Ellenson reports the moving figures as "engaged in rapid, furtive movement past doorways or windows, reflected in a mirror, or darting behind furniture." The figures are seen by survivors directly or through their peripheral vision, and are "seldom seen when the [survivor is] away from home."

The auditory hallucinations and sounds fall into two categories: "intruder" and "vocal sounds." Common examples of intruder sounds are: "footsteps, breathing, scrapes, doorknobs turning, doors opening and closing, windows being tampered with." The intruder sounds, like the images, occur most often at night when the survivor is in bed.

Vocal sounds sometimes occur to a survivor as the voice of a child in distress, "calling the name of a parent or a noun like 'mommy' . . ."

Other auditory hallucinations fall into three groups: 1) persecutory, 2) directive, and 3) inner helper voices. "Persecutory voices," Ellenson writes, "condemned the survivor in sexual terms, calling her 'whore,' 'bitch,' and 'slut.' They told her that she was no good, that she was garbage. . . . Directive voices goaded a few survivors towards physical mistreatment of themselves, suicide, or outward acts of violence. . . . Inner helper voices attempted to soothe a few survivors with such phrases as, 'It is going to be okay' . . . (and) sometimes defended the client to the persecutors. . . .

"It is very rare," Ellenson continues, "for the survivor to reveal the presence of perceptual disturbances spontaneously. Over and over . . . the author asked if the survivor had ever revealed these symptoms before. Frequently, the answer was 'No . . . Because I thought I would be called crazy.' "

AMNESIA

The first symptom you may have to address is whether you have amnesia for any periods of your childhood. Even if you know that there are amnesiac episodes, you may not know yet what occurred during these periods. Remember that identifying a period of amnesia from your childhood or adolescence does not necessarily mean you are an incest survivor. What it does typically indicate is that there was some kind of trauma occurring during this period that has not been resolved.

It is useful during this stage to hear other survivors' stories, to wear away at possible memory repression. Don't expect to do it all at once. The slow process of breaking denial, of working through the amnesia, can be frustrating. But it may be beneficial, even necessary. The psyche knows when it is ready to handle information that has been suppressed. It may wait until your support system is strong enough before allowing the information to come to your conscious memory. Through the process of educating yourself about the signs and symptoms of incest, you may gradually come to identify yourself as a survivor.

PROCESSES TO WORK ON AMNESIA

Answer the following questions to the best of your ability. If you don't feel a question applies to you at this time, simply move on to the next one. Although many survivors experience similar residual effects of childhood abuse, everyone has her own unique experience and recovery process. If you have no amnesia that you can identify, move on to the next section, "Processes to Identify 'Splitting Off,' " and come back to this process if it seems appropriate later on.

1. Are there periods in your childhood that seem foggy, vague, or altogether blank? Are there periods you can remember clearly before and afterward?

_____

2. Can you find any pictures of yourself or your family during these periods? Look at them gently and slowly, allowing yourself time to muse over them. See if the pictures stir any feelings or images in you. Write down your thoughts and feelings. _____

_____

3. Can you remember any songs from time periods that you don't remember? What happens when you hear music that was popular when you were a child, preadolescent, and/or teenager? _____

_____

17

4. Do you have any family members you could talk to about these amnesiac periods (particularly family members who might be sensitive to you and your search)? Ask them if you can talk to them about their memories of your family during these periods. Collect their stories and recollections about what you were like as a child.

PROCESSES TO IDENTIFY "SPLITTING OFF"

Look over the following list of questions. Answer the questions by writing down whatever comes to your mind first:

1. Do you ever notice yourself "checking out," "splitting off," or "going numb"?

_____

2. Begin to track your tendency to split off. How long did you "leave" for? Days, weeks, hours, minutes? What was going on right before you left? Is there anything in that experience that might have been a "trigger"—in other words, that might have precipitated it?

_____

_____

3. Identify your memory triggers. Do any experiences in your life make you feel out-of-control, shaky, weak in the knees, dizzy, or short of breath? Do any give you heart palpitations, clammy palms, or make you feel as if you're going to faint or start screaming or crying? Do you have panic attacks?

_____

_____

Do you have recurring bad dreams? What are the themes or what is the story?

_____

_____

4. Define your memory triggers. What are the experiences that were occurring right before you had a panic attack or went numb?

_____

_____

Do you react to certain smells, sounds, touches, and/or visual stimuli? Examples: smelling men's cologne or alcohol on someone's breath; sounds of screaming or glass breaking; being in enclosed spaces such as elevators, movie theaters, or rows of chairs?

19

What are your preferences and dislikes of touch? Do you hate to be hugged, or are there areas of your body that you feel an aversion to? What are your sensations around having anything in your mouth or throat (during dental work, etc.)?

What are your feelings when you see male and female genitalia in different contexts? What feels okay and what feels bad? Does anything feel horrible or repulsive?

How do you react to lighting, different room sizes, different volumes of sounds? What movies do you have strong emotional reactions to? What are the movies' themes and content, and what is the visual stimuli?

_____

_____

PROCESS FOR IDENTIFYING YOURSELF AS A SURVIVOR

Go over the following list and check off the questions that register a response in you. This list is not conclusive, nor does it definitively identify you as an incest survivor. Many of the items are also symptoms of other experiences. If you have any of the following symptoms, it may be a clue that you are an incest survivor; if you have several symptoms, there is an increased likelihood. You are the only person who can make the final determination.

_____ 1. Do you remember a parent, adult, or sibling touching you in any way that felt sexual, bad, or scary to you as a child?

_____ 2. Do you know of any history of incest or sexual abuse in your parents' or siblings' childhoods?

_____ 3. Do you have memories of physical abuse or neglect in your childhood? Do you have amnesia or memory loss about any periods of your childhood?

_____ 4. Do you have intrusive memories or flashbacks of incidents that are traumatic to you? Do you have repetitive traumatic dreams?

_____ 5. Do you experience "startle response," a tendency to feel hypersensitive to your environment, either regularly or in response to certain stimuli (people, smells, sounds, movies, etc.)?

_____ 6. Are either of your parents alcoholic or addicted to drugs?

_____ 7. If your parents are divorced, did you spend much time with a single parent? Was it your opposite-sexed parent? Did the single parent have partners in his or her life, and, if so, what was your relationship with them? Were you raised by extended family members such as grandparents, aunts, or uncles?

_____ 8. Do you have a sense of shame about yourself or your body? Do you feel your body is ugly or are you uncomfortable taking your clothes off?

_____ 9. Do you repeatedly go to bed fully clothed? Did you as a child?

_____ **10.** Do you feel a distaste about sex or your own sexuality?

_____ **11.** Do you have thoughts/feelings about being bad or dirty?

_____ **12.** Do you "check out," "leave your body," go numb, or experience yourself as a spectator frequently, especially during sex?

_____ **13.** Do you see sex as the only or primary way to get what you need from a partner?

_____ **14.** Do you experience a sense of evil or doom, either in a specific or general and pervasive way?

_____ **15.** Do you experience a "flooding" of feelings of rage or fear? Do you have "panic reactions"?

_____ **16.** Do you choose abusive partners for relationships—people who are chemically dependent, emotionally unavailable, violent, or very needy? Have any of your partners been sexual abuse survivors or perpetrators?

_____ **17.** Do you have an eating disorder or are you chemically dependent?

_____ **18.** Do you self-mutilate—cut, burn, pick at yourself, or fantasize a lot about hurting yourself? What are the fantasies? Are you accident-prone, either all the time or periodically?

_____ **19.** Do you have various unidentifiable physical problems that doctors can't seem to solve? Have you had any unnecessary surgeries?

_____ **20.** Do you have fears about getting "closed in" (for example, sitting in the middle of a group with no easy exit, choking, suffocating, fears of commitment in relationships)? Do you feel that anybody really knows you? Do you feel as if you are enclosed behind a wall or that there's always a veil between you and others?

After you've checked off those symptoms that apply to you, go back and count up how many questions registered some kind of response in yourself and write down the numbers here.

_____

Look over those questions again and write down any images or memories that came to you as you read them.

FURTHER PROCESSES TO WORK ON

If you're ready to do some deeper exploration of your memories, add the following questions to the above list for a more thorough review:

1. For which periods of your life do you have no memory? Do you know anything about what was going on in the family during these periods?

_____

2. What do you know about the history of sexual abuse in your family? Were your parents, stepparents, or siblings ever molested? What are the stories or bits of stories that you've heard? What are your parents' reactions when you

ask them questions about their childhoods? Is there a
refusal to talk? What's the emotional tone of their
response to your questioning?

_____

3. What are the memories of physical abuse or neglect in
your childhood? _____

4. What is the content of your intrusive memories,
flashbacks, or recurring dreams? What happens?

_____

5. What triggers your "startle response"? ___ _____

_____

6. Which parent is addicted and what is the duration of
their substance abuse? How far back does it go?

_____

7. What are your memories of how you spent time alone
with your parenting figures? During that time, what was
the physical and emotional contact like? _____

_____

8. Do you have a Critical Voice or a part of you that calls
you bad names or constantly berates you? What does it
say? _____

9. Do you feel depressed or as if you have no energy?

_____

10. Do you feel different than others in a negative way? This may be a vague feeling, but try to make it as specific as possible. What is it about yourself that is so bad? What have you done or thought about that is so horrible? Can you let others get close to you? Who do you feel is closest to you? Can you allow them to be with you when you're feeling bad?

_____

11. How do you feel about your body? _____

_____

What do you do to "check out" of it? _____

_____

What do you do to take care of it? _____

_____

Are you obsessed with or do you have any strong negative feelings about any specific parts of your or others' bodies? Which parts? What are the feelings?

_____

12. What are your memories of going to bed fully clothed? What feelings did or do you have about going to bed at night?

_____

13. What are your feelings about having sex? Do you "leave" during sex? Do you feel compulsive about sex?

_____

Do you ever have feelings of being worthless and as if life has no meaning when you go through periods of being nonsexual? _____

_____

_____

If you're in a sexual relationship, try to gently increase your awareness of yourself during sex. If it feels safe, communicate with your partner if you notice yourself starting to "leave." See Chapter Six for a longer discussion on "Recovering Sexuality."

14. Do you now have or have you ever had an eating disorder? _____

Are you a compulsive overeater? _____

Are you bulimic? Do you throw up or use other methods to purge food after eating? _____

Are you anorexic? Do you starve yourself or have cycles of bingeing and starving? _____

Do you exercise compulsively? Do you get depressed or very anxious about your body if you can't go to aerobics class or do other exercise rituals? _____

If you can't stop overeating by yourself, it's very important to get help. The following is a list of support systems for eating disorders for you to consider:

Hospital programs

Eating disorder therapy groups

Individual therapy

Overeaters Anonymous

See chapters Two and Three for more information about where to get help and how to begin recovery from compulsive behaviors.

15. Describe your panic attacks. What are the periods of "flooding feelings" like? What kinds of feelings do you get flooded with? How long do these periods last?

_____

_____

16. Describe your fantasies of hurting yourself. What have you done to hurt yourself? _____

There is often a coded message in the fantasy material you have. Because it may contain information or suppress it, it can be very valuable to look at. Try to use an observing, nonjudgmental viewpoint to see what it contains and whether there are any clues in it.

17. Do you self-mutilate? Do you cut, burn, or hurt yourself? What do you do? Have you ever had to seek medical treatment for it? _____

Does anybody know you do this? What does it feel like to talk about this? How does it feel to have these questions asked of you? Do you feel fear or shame about revealing this to someone?

_____

If you answer yes to question 17, seek professional help immediately. Some part of you is screaming for help, and it's very important to get another human being to help you with it. You're not bad—this is a coping mechanism. Everyone always has very good reasons for everything they do. Like many obsessive-compulsive disorders, self-mutilation is often an attempt to contain or bind feelings— usually of overwhelming pain or rage. However, it is dangerous to allow this symptom to go unchecked.

The next step is learning how to derail the thought. Like a train going downhill, the more self-destructive thoughts you allow yourself to hold onto, the more powerful they will become. How can you interrupt it? What can you substitute for it? For processes on compulsive-obsessive disorders, see Chapter Three.

PROCESSES FOR CONTACTING AND CLARIFYING MEMORIES

Often a woman asks, "How do I recover if I don't have clear picture memories?" Many survivors have a sense that some kind of sexual abuse occurred although they have no exact picture of it. Others describe an odd, elusive feeling of foreboding, shame, fear of men, and so on, with no exact reason for these feelings that makes sense to them.

If you don't have clear picture memories, it's probably a good idea to keep exposing yourself to information about incest and to other survivors in various stages of their recovery. When a memory does appear, write it down and/ or call someone who is sensitive and supportive of your recovery. Tell them what's going on with you—don't just talk about the weather. Recording your memories is important because if you go back into denial or the memory disappears, you will have some lasting evidence of what you experienced. Often women get fragments of memories that, over time, gradually form a collage-like picture of the incest.

At some point, things will get clearer. In the meantime, some activities that may help are:

1. Reading books (especially about other women's stories).

Outgrowing the Pain, by Eliana Gill

Incest and Sexuality: A Guide to Understanding and Healing, by Wendy Maltz and Beverly Holman

Courage to Heal, by Ellen Bass and Laura Davis

Whiskey's Song, by Mitzi Chandler

Triumph over Darkness, by Wendy Wood and Leslie Hatton

I Never Told Anyone, by Ellen Bass

My Father's House: A Memoir of Incest and Healing, by Sylvia Fraser

Betrayal of Innocence, by Susan Forward

Emotional Child Abuse, by Joel D. Covitz

Reclaiming Our Lives, by Carol Poston and Karen Lison

Secret Scars, by Cynthia Tower

2. Attending lectures and groups.

(See Chapter Two for a description of types of groups.)

3. Journal writing.

A journal can be your best friend during this time. It is always available in a way people may not be. Developing the habit of getting feelings out of yourself and of putting words to feelings is very important. Journal writing may be a good stepping-stone to becoming able to share feelings with another person. It is not true that some people are better at talking and self-disclosure than others—they just have more practice.

4. Dream work.

Keep a dream journal and pen by your bed and write down your dreams as soon as you wake up. Sometimes just by focusing on your dreams, you will begin to remember more. Some people report being able to program themselves before falling asleep, so that it's easier to remember their dreams when they awaken. Others find that when they set an alarm to wake up and then go back to sleep for a short time before waking up, they dream vividly.

5. Going to movies.

Proceed carefully with this; visual stimulation can be highly confrontive. Because visual stimulation is so powerful and able to cut through your mental defenses, watching movies sometimes propels you back in time. If, during or after the movie, you find yourself feeling like the little child who was being hurt, use it as an opportunity to get in touch with those feelings. If possible, have a supportive friend or partner watch the movie with you so that if feelings do come up, you'll have someone to support you and bring you back to the present. Some possibilities of movies are:

Nuts

Something About Amelia—NBC Movie of the Week

To a Safer Place: A Story of Healing of Incest

Breaking Silence

6. Hypnosis.

This is not highly recommended by some therapists, except as a last resort, because generally your unconscious releases repressed memories in its own time —usually when you have created enough safety in your life and have a good, strong support system to adequately handle the memory. However, if a therapist is experienced with incest issues and is trained in hypnotherapy, it can be an excellent vehicle to access previously irretrievable memories and unlock the amnesia. Just be sure you are going to a safe place after your session and that you make time to process the feelings accompanying your memories. It is important not to retraumatize yourself by pushing or digging for memories.

GRACE'S STORY

Introduction

The following is one woman's story of her abuse and recovery, told in her own words.

Grace tells about her childhood abuse and how it affected her beliefs and self-image. She describes the long-term effects of the incest, which include many of the symptoms identified as Post-traumatic Stress Disorder: amnesia, startle response, phobias, and intrusive images when exposed to a memory trigger. Grace also talks about what has changed in her life as a result of the help she has received for the incest, what happened when she broke through the amnesia and began to retrieve her memories, and how her relationships and self-esteem have changed in recovery.

Grace's is one of five survivor stories presented in this book. They are given at length to demonstrate the diverse but interwoven patterns and cycles of abuse, its long-term effects and, most importantly, the issues each woman faced in her recovery, what she found helpful and what she accomplished. My hope is that these stories will aid you by allowing you to see what feelings or memories they may trigger for you. For example, how are you similar to Grace? How are you different? If you don't identify with any elements of this or other stories, note that down, too.

A retired health care professional in her fifties, Grace is married and the mother of four grown children. As the only child of parents who divorced when she was seven, she was raised alternately by her grandmother, mother, and father with his mistress.

Grace's molestation by her father, an alcoholic, began when she was very young, possibly age two, and continued until she was seventeen. The molestation included fondling, oral sex, and possibly intercourse.

Memories of her early physical and sexual abuse were entirely repressed until Grace was forty-two years old and in therapy with a psychiatrist who hypnotized her. In the beginning, the memories seemed more like a dream to her than the remembering of actual events. As time went on, more memories emerged, along with explanations for symptoms she had struggled with for a long time but had not understood, such as an inability to have her feet touched (with an accompanying memory of having her feet tied), and waking up in a rage if her husband's body touched hers during sleep.

As her understanding of her experience grew, Grace was able to see more and more that she had always felt the effects of the abuse without knowing it: She had always experienced a feeling of never being safe, of evil lurking around her; she had always been a vomiter; and she panicked when she had to have anything in her mouth.

Grace's recovery has taken many years and a lot of patience. She has many phobias and still experiences confusion about her perceptions of reality. Like many survivors, Grace had asked for help as a child, only to find that the people she reached out to were either unwilling to believe her or to do anything to help her. Although married for thirty-four years, she carried a sense of herself as bad, worthless, and unlovable. She found it difficult to allow herself sexual pleasure, but recently, with the help of her husband, she is making progress.

Grace's Story

This scene came to me in what I thought had been a dream. My therapist, however, said it was a memory because it was so detailed: I had a view from up in a corner, and I was watching my mother and father in the kitchen having a fight. We lived in a rural area, and my mother was cooking on a wood stove. My father grabbed the skillet and threw it out in the backyard. My mother left, and I could see myself coloring with crayons, thinking if I was very quiet and could concentrate very hard on the coloring, maybe nobody would notice me. I knew when my mother left, my father would come for me. Next I see him leading me by the hand to the bedroom, and I can hear screaming. I thought when I first had the recall that it was my mother screaming, but later I came to know it was me. Something happened that day I still haven't remembered, but it was so awful that I learned not to scream ever again.

I don't know how long or how many times the incest occurred with my father, but I know it was through the first seven years of my life. When I was seven, my parents divorced and I didn't see my father again until I was twelve. Interestingly, those are the years I don't remember, seven to twelve.

Once I ran away to my grandmother's house. My grandmother's reaction must have been something very bad because I never ran away again. So there was nobody to keep me safe.

That's been a recurring theme in my life: I'll never be safe. For me, evil is free-floating, although it has dimensions. It only comes when I'm around. If I step out my front door, evil will come down; if I stay in and it doesn't find me, the whole world will be safe. Evil has always had a reality for me. It has personification; it is not an idea, it is a thing that knows me.

Other memories of my childhood are of my mother hitting me. I can see her hand coming down in the crib, but I am out of my body and I see her hitting a little child. My mother cut twelve switches from the peach trees every day because she said I was such a bad child, she knew she'd need them. They used to have a joke that the peach orchard would never grow because of me.

My grandmother put me in a drawstring bag and tied it to the foot of the bed. I have a hunch this had gone on for generations because I remember stories that my uncle used to carry a little penknife around with him so he could cut himself out of the bag. My clearest memory of why she did it to me was because I was catching June bugs and tying a string to their legs.

After the divorce both my parents left and I was placed with my grandmother. I thought that everything that happened was my fault and I felt completely abandoned. This crystallized my feeling that I was bad and worthless. I thought that if I could just be good enough, I could prevent something terrible from happening. With the divorce, my worst fear of being abandoned for being "bad" had materialized, despite my efforts, and I was hopeless.

My mother allowed me to see my father again when I was twelve. For the first two years he made no overt sexual advance, but there was a background theme that I was the only one who really loved him, that I'd keep house for him. It felt inappropriate. The implication was, "You're for me and the two of us should be together and make this little nest."

When I was in college my father would come to see me. Sometimes he'd pick me up to go to a football game. We'd go with another couple who were his friends. One day we were riding in the car, and the other man and his mistress were in the frontseat; they were drunk and feeling each other. My father and I were in the backseat, and he turned to me and put his arms around me and began to French kiss me. He was acting like we were two couples out on a date except that he was my father. He made passes at some of my college friends, too. I lost one friend over that.

About this time, I began to realize that my father was an alcoholic. His boss would call me to help get him sober. One time, I went to rescue my father in another state where he was working. My father came into my hotel room that night and began to fondle me and then tried to have intercourse with me. It was the first time he made a direct frontal attempt. I fought him off. I guess he was weak because of the alcohol or the detox because he gave up after a while.

I got him committed to a treatment center, and went back to his mistress and told her what happened. She was angry. I remember her saying, "That bastard!" but she was his "enabler" (co-alcoholic), and she didn't really do anything about it. I was so exhausted by this point, I just had to tell somebody.

I finally told him never to see me again unless he was really willing to be a father to me. That was the last time I saw him alive. I think it was my last plea for what I really needed.

Years later I finally sought help in therapy, and the incest memories came up during hypnosis. When the memories started surfacing, I thought I was going to choke or throw up. I realized I was remembering an oral sexual event. I wasn't certain that I knew what I was remembering; I didn't want to believe it. The therapist was very helpful; he had thought for a long time that there had been incest in my past, and there was nothing in his face or voice tone that doubted me, which I think was very important. So it was like seeing two parallel processes occurring at the same time: I could see the experience and see myself seeing the experience. Yet I still had to deny it.

Then memories would sweep over me for some years. I'd be driving and need to pull over because I'd feel like I was going to throw up. I would be on my way to work in traffic in a tight space and a memory would take over and I'd think, "I can't pull off." I'd feel panicky. Eventually, I learned to control the need to throw up.

As I understood it more, I began to piece some things together about my life. I'd always been a vomiter; at the dentist, I'd go into a panic any time I had to have something put in my mouth, like that stuff they leave in to make an impression for a night guard. If I was put under anesthesia, I'd always be throwing up and throwing up. I knew it was bizarre and part of me still thinks I made it up.

At certain points in my therapy, I'd say, "If incest is so prevalent, why am I making such a big deal out of it?" I remember my therapist saying, "Death was prevalent in the prison camps, too. That didn't make it all right."

I was still making excuses for my father, saying he

must have been molested as a child. I could never get angry at him until years later. It was not until my father died that a great rage swept over me. I think my fear of losing his love or of what would happen to me if anybody ever knew how angry I was, was so great, I could not be aware of my anger toward him while he was alive.

Before the memories came up, I'd get a recurring image of my father lying face down, drunk and passed out on the bed, and I'd see me hiding in the corner. I could see this blonde-headed girl peering out, and I'd get this feeling of "Oh, he's done it again." I'd sometimes see my mother entering the room, and I'd realize she'd left me with him and something awful had happened. Another thing I began to know was that my feet had been tied, or that he had held my feet with his hands. To this day, if I'm lying down or if my feet are on a footstool and somebody passes by and touches my feet, I get crazy.

During the night if my husband would throw his arm over me while he was sleeping or if my body would roll into his while I was sleeping I'd go into a wild rage. Sometimes I'd wake up to find myself taking my hands, chopping and chopping at him, trying to kill him. I wanted to be able to sleep closer to him, just sleep, not even be sexual, so we worked on this together and it's getting easier.

At this time in my life, sometimes I just want a hug and I feel like I'm surrounded by a Plexiglas wall. Sometimes I feel like I need to chop that whole part of myself away and not even try to be sexual.

My therapist worked with me on knowing that as a

child, at the beginning of the encounter with my father, I'd felt pleasure before something else happened that was terrifying. So sexuality was a predicament for me; pleasure was dangerous and followed by terror. My therapist gave me permission to have felt the pleasure initially, so now, if I can feel a little pleasure and let it be good, the wall doesn't always have to come up.

There are lots of good changes in my life due to the incest survivor recovery work I've done. One of the changes is that even when I get depressed, it feels different. I still get bad feelings and want to hide my body parts and sexuality; I feel embarrassed about how I look. I wish people dressed like Amish people so I could stay covered up. But I understand I have choices and coping skills and can do something about it when I'm ready. I can ask my partner for help if he's willing. We made progress when we worked on the learning to allow touch while I'm sleeping. I used to wake up in a panic attack if any part of his body was touching me. I've decided if I can master it 75 percent of the time, it's okay. Lately, I've found that I sometimes have actually felt comfort and pleasure in waking up and wanting to be held by my husband while we're sleeping. After being married for thirty-four years we are making some progress toward intimacy.

As I look back over my parenting years, I see that I had the belief that children are supposed to please parents. I still don't know what being a good parent is. I have a fantasy about it being a person who keeps a child safe and protects them. What a parent is and what a person is are all scrambled in my mind. I still don't have very good boundaries, and I feel I must fix other people because that's my role.

It's also very hard for me to stand unflinchingly by my own truth. I try to state, "This is a fact," but if anyone takes issue with me, I doubt my own perception. I was so drilled to accept a lie when I knew it wasn't the truth, because everybody pretended the incest wasn't happening even when I openly asked for help.

It has taken me fifty-seven years to know I am really a good and wonderful lady, but fifty-seven years is a long time to live feeling like a victim. A lot of situations in my life came about because I was running away from the incest memories and believing I had to take care of everybody.

I feel blessed to be able to put these memories into words, piecing them together like a puzzle, bit by bit. I believe it's freeing me to "be present" in my life for the first time and enjoy the moment. Some of the fears and hypervigilance are easing up a little. I can accept and respect my husband for who he is rather than always guarding myself from him. We go on dates and we're learning to play together—just doing simple things like taking walks and holding hands, flying kites and defining mutual interests. I feel like my life is opening up and I'm slowly learning to trust that things will just keep getting better and better.

Notes on your reaction to Grace's Story:

What parts triggered something in you? Was there anything that you related to or that brought back memories? Was there anything you had a negative reaction to? Do you know why?

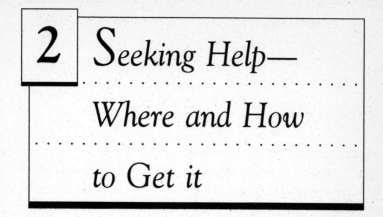

2 | Seeking Help—
Where and How
to Get it

Recovery from sexual abuse and emotional incest is not a solitary process; it requires that you "open up" to allow others to give you the help and support you need. This assistance will come in many different forms and from many different sources; what they are and how to go about bringing them into your life will be the subject of this chapter.

As a survivor, you may discover that seeking help is a completely foreign concept to you. Your survival has depended on cutting yourself off from your own needs and keeping them a secret from others at all costs. However, there will come a point when you simply must reach out because you can't go any further without bringing another human being into your healing process.

Seeking help consists of several activities, including gathering information, identifying resources, building your own support system, and entering therapy.

Taking the necessary steps one at a time will help you to overcome any resistance you may feel about it. The processes given in this chapter also will assist you.

INFORMATION GATHERING

Begin by simply collecting information. As we've seen in Chapter One, the most important information you need will come from you: Take time to learn about yourself and what you need. Listen to your feelings and thoughts. What people and resources do you want in your life? Whom can you feel good about letting in? Whom do you want to help you? Keep working on your journal writing and dream work—these are important ways to keep in touch with what your feelings are. (See the "Process for Contacting Feelings" at the end of Chapter Three.)

Another area of internal fact collecting will be an assessment of whether you need more information on the signs and symptoms of incest to help you identify yourself as a survivor. Here, too, your journal and dream work will prove helpful, but you can also find additional information through reading books, attending lectures, seeing movies, and talking with others who are survivors or who deal with recovery issues.

In addition to internal fact collecting, you may want to find out what kinds of help are available in your community.

IDENTIFYING RESOURCES

"Resources" here means any organized source of help and support. Those that will be discussed in this chapter include community organizations, support systems, and therapy.

COMMUNITY ORGANIZATIONS

Crisis Units and Mental Health Services

Most communities offer outpatient counseling services through a county mental health clinic that usually also includes a crisis unit or inpatient hospital unit. Being an outpatient client means you see a counselor for individual or group therapy for one to two hours a week. Being an inpatient means you have the option of staying overnight and having counselors available to you twenty-four hours a day. Typical inpatient stays range from one day to a few weeks.

Church Groups

For some survivors, church groups provide a sober community of supportive people who are nurturing and comforting. However, when choosing any support community, keep in mind that you should be able to address your experiences and feelings honestly, without judgment or blame from anyone.

Self-Help Groups

In my experience, survivors have found self-help groups that are specifically involved in recovery issues to be the most valuable to their recovery. These include Parents United and the Twelve Step programs.

Parents United is a national organization with chapters in most major cities. Led by trained facilitators and therapists, Parents United group meetings are available for Adults Molested as Children, Perpetrators, and Partners of Survivors. Their structure resembles other self-help groups, but the therapists associated with Parents United generally have received some training specific to incest recovery. Parents United meetings may be just once a week and have a minimal donation, such as five dollars.

Incest Survivors Anonymous and Adult Children of Alcoholics (ACA) are two examples of Twelve Step programs that offer open meetings in virtually all areas of the country. All the so-called anonymous or Twelve Step programs are entirely self-help oriented. Developed from the principles of recovery formulated in Alcoholics Anonymous (AA), these programs have now been adapted to a wide range of issues, including Incest Survivors Anonymous, Narcotics Anonymous, Parents Anonymous (for parents who may abuse their children), Overeaters Anonymous, Gamblers Anonymous, Sex and Love Addicts Anonymous, Co-dependents Anonymous, Arts Anonymous (for artists who sabotage their creative expression), and Debtors Anonymous. All Twelve Step programs offer an excellent support system, and many members make themselves available to newcomers twenty-four hours a day. The meetings are often held in public meeting places, such as churches, libraries, and schools.

These self-help groups are "anonymous" because no one shares their last name, and what you see and hear at meetings does not leave these meetings. This is the basis of trust upon which the fellowship operates. There is nothing to sign; there are no leaders, no dues or fees. So even if you're not sure if you belong, you can ask where the open meetings are and just go to a few to listen to the stories and discussions to see if you identify with them.

Most meetings begin with a speaker who talks for about half an hour about his or her active addiction and recovery. Then a half-hour discussion follows during which people in the group volunteer to share their thoughts and experiences. You don't have to introduce yourself if you don't want to and you don't have to talk to anyone. You can sit in the back of the room and check it out for a while. People may offer you their phone numbers, particularly if you choose to introduce yourself as a newcomer. This gives you the chance to sort out your questions with someone on a one-to-one basis if you're not comfortable sharing on a group level. In many groups, there is an informal tradition of going out to coffee after the meeting, which allows for more idea sharing.

In addition to attending meetings, many people seeking recovery through one (or more) of the anonymous programs work through a series of processes for recovery known as the Twelve Steps. Each of the steps addresses specific core issues one must confront and resolve in recovery. Working the steps is an individual process; people vary as to how quickly they proceed through them. My version of the Twelve Steps, adapted specifically to incest survivor issues, appears at the end of this chapter.

Much of the personal support you may gain from an anonymous group will come from your sponsor. A sponsor is an individual who has been in recovery long enough to have achieved a measure of stability and understanding of her own recovery process and that of others. She has probably worked through the Twelve Steps and can assist you in working yours. Your sponsor can answer any questions you have about the issues you are confronting and provide the emotional support you need but that you don't feel comfortable requesting from the group. It is recommended that women work with women and men with men, but there are no rules in Twelve Step programs, only suggestions.

To find a meeting, look in the yellow pages under "Alcoholics Anonymous," "Al-Anon/Adult Children of Alcoholics Family Groups," or the names of other anonymous groups. Write down the number, call and ask for information on Incest Survivors Anonymous, ACA meetings, and/or Parents United meetings. There is usually a Twelve Step meeting every day of the week (depending on the size of your city and geographic area). Most major cities have meetings going on almost every hour of the day from 6:00 A.M. until midnight. Many cities also have Twelve Step clubhouses where recovering people meet to have coffee and talk or play cards. In some areas, local newspapers run meeting information in the "personals" sections.

PROCESSES FOR CONTACTING
COMMUNITY SELF-HELP GROUPS

Parents United or Twelve Step program name

_____

Phone number _____

Time and day of meeting _____

Location _____

Directions _____

Can someone call you back (if it's an answering service),
or meet you at the meeting, if you'd like that?

_____

SUPPORT SYSTEMS

Your support system begins with friends and acquain-
tances and can be expanded to include your therapist,
various support or therapy groups, and other people
in your life.

You may begin recovery feeling isolated or without
a reliable support system. This is typical of survivors.
Many survivors have had limited opportunities to develop friendships as children. They had to keep the
family secret or be the mother to the entire family
because of their assignment to the wife or adult role.
Sometimes survivors have been prohibited from
spending time with boys because of inappropriate pa-
rental jealousy. Sometimes they have been prevented

from spending time with other little girls—and later, adult women—because of their shame.

Developing bonding relationships and creating a support system is a progressive process, and it takes time. Many survivors arrive at adulthood feeling totally lost about how to go about connecting with other people, particularly without using sex, drugs, or alcohol to initiate the contact. Social skills can be learned—it's just a matter of practice and persistence. We will return to this subject at greater length in later chapters.

There is an important distinction to be made between emotional support—such as your friends can provide—and professional help from a therapist. Friends can provide special support by being willing to listen to your feelings and respond sensitively. At times friends are better than therapists and other professionals because they can spend time with you or be available by phone, even at odd hours. They may care about you and support you in a special way. This is very beneficial and important.

Usually, however, friends lack the professional training and insight that therapists have. A therapist possesses special skills to lead you to your own insights, to help you to pace yourself at getting in touch with and expressing your feelings, so that you can handle them. It's the therapist's job to lead you through your blocks and to create a safe place and relationship so that you can open up.

Another difference between therapists and friends is that friends usually want your attention and support in return. Reciprocation is a healthy expectation for a friendship. But, if you go through a period where you need to relive some old feelings from your childhood, you may not have the energy or inclination to give anything to anyone. This will pass, but until then you need to give yourself permission to experience some of the pain and anger you suppressed as a child and give yourself some time to feel needy. You are undertaking the stages you missed in childhood.

It is perfectly acceptable and necessary for children to have a focus on "self," yet most survivors had to skip this developmental stage because of inappropriate demands by their parents. Being an incest survivor probably meant you had to sacrifice your own sense of self to attend to the "needy child" of the parent. In recovery, you need some relationships where it is okay for you to be feeling your grief, anger, and neediness. If you can honor the feelings instead of "stuffing" them down, they will dissipate and lighten up. Eventually, this will allow you to give to others in relationships in a whole different way—to give because you want to and not because you have to.

In some unusual cases, family members can be a source of support, but this is the exception and not the rule. Incest is always a family issue and typically brings up either very strong feelings or lots of denial. Usually survivors need to avoid their families during certain periods of their recovery, particularly when the feelings are raw and right on the surface. The power of family rules is very strong; there are usually unspoken injunctions in incestuous families to "go unconscious" and deny what the rest of the family doesn't see. Children always know, on some level, if

their parents are hurting, and there is an overwhelming pull to maintain loyalty and not upset the family
system. However, family members who have been in
therapy or are in their own recovery may be able to
lend you valuable support.

THERAPY

In most cases survivors need to have a guide who has
some professional training and experience with the
therapeutic process. This is because there are times
when direct interventions need to be made to allow
you to release information or feelings that you can't
get to on your own. An example of a direct intervention is the pursuit of a line of questioning designed
to lead you into your feelings. Another intervention
is watching the way you tighten your muscles in your
jaw or throat to avoid crying about something painful
and asking you to do some breathing rather than
"holding in" the feelings.

Entering Therapy

A relationship with a therapist is different than a
friendship because you have no obligation to take care
of your therapist. You don't have to know anything
about your therapist's personal life, or worry about
or listen to his or her problems. Your therapist's job
is to devote his or her full attention to you during the
course of your session. In doing so, the therapist is in

effect providing the parenting that was missing during your childhood. When you allow yourself to receive this attention and support, you can begin to internalize a Good Parent into yourself and become your own source of comfort, nurture, and self-affirmation.

Your therapist's office is the place for you to feel your feelings; you don't have to spend a lot of time keeping up social graces. You are allowed to rely on your therapist and let yourself "fall apart" if you need to. There is a different level of commitment in a therapy relationship on both the therapist's and the client's parts; your therapist doesn't cancel your time together because he or she gets busy with something else. Both of you agree to show up at a specific time on a specific day, every week, and to keep it a priority, until it is no longer needed.

When choosing a therapist, some survivors know they want their therapist to be a woman, and/or a recovering survivor herself. For others, an emotional tone of strength and a sense of calm are the most important qualities in selecting a good person to work with, rather than the gender or background of the person.

Aspects of Therapy Found Useful to Survivors

A big part of the incest survivor healing process is to experience being in a safe place and in a relationship where it's safe to have feelings, where you are believed, where you feel hope, and where you receive closure. Closure is the experience of "being put back together again" after experiencing strong emotions. For example, if you've been crying, it's important to have time to slow down and get centered before you return to activity. A good, caring therapist can provide all of this.

Individual Versus Group Therapy: Which to Choose?

Some survivors elect to be in both individual and group therapy because they can enhance each other.

If you have never been to therapy before, it might be a good idea to do at least six months of individual therapy so that you can really focus on yourself and your feelings and go over your history step by step. However, if it feels too frightening to get close to one person, or if you feel more comfortable being around other survivors, you may prefer working in a group.

The benefit of individual therapy is that you can experience a dependable bond with one person and receive attention and support just for you. You also have the opportunity to work through fears and blocks about bonding, trusting, and receiving in a way that isn't as intense in a group. If you're not very assertive or a good communicator, you may get lost in a group if the therapist or other group members don't draw you out. In individual therapy, you can't distract yourself from your own issues by being a caretaker to someone else, although some people feel they can "hide out" or even manipulate an individual therapist in a way they can't a whole group.

The benefits of being in group therapy are: the opportunity to identify with other survivors who may be a little further along in identifying their memories and feelings, which may help to trigger yours; the chance to trust several people, some of whom may become a part of your social/emotional support system; and, for survivors with authority fears, group therapy is less threatening because it feels as if everyone is on the same level. Group therapy is typically less expensive.

PROCESSES FOR CHOOSING A THERAPIST OR THERAPY GROUP

To find a therapist for individual therapy, begin by talking to people you respect who have any connection, personally or professionally, to the counseling field and ask for recommendations. If that's not possible, look in the yellow pages under "Counseling," "Psychotherapists," "Psychologists," "Women's Centers," "Rape Crisis Centers," "Sexual Trauma Centers," and so on. Write the numbers below:

_____

Make calls and ask for information on a therapist or counselor who specializes in incest survivor recovery.

To locate therapy groups, look up the following organizations in the phone book to see if they have any local chapters in your area:

Child Protective Services

Rape/Sexual Trauma Crisis Center

Abused Women's Services

Women's Therapy Referral Network

These organizations have access to information on therapy groups for all different kinds of women's issues, and they may know about a group for incest survivors.

Taking this step is one of the hardest parts of recovery. You might find yourself "going unconscious" even during the process of considering calling a therapist. So keep a pad of paper with you and write down names, numbers, leads, and fees for several different therapists.

You may have to talk to an intake worker first. If possible, talk to the recommended therapists by phone and ask them how they work. How do you feel when you are talking with each one? Who feels safe to you? Check credentials and ask about their personal recovery, and their philosophy and treatment methods, if they are willing to discuss them.

Name/address/phone number of agency or therapist

_____

Group or individual _____

I talked to: (name) _____ (title) _____

$ per session _____

Available times to meet _____

Date of initial consultation _____

Name/address/phone number of agency or therapist

_____

Group or individual _____

I talked to: (name) _____ (title) _____

$ per session _____

Available times to meet _____

Date of initial consultation _____

Name/address/phone number of agency or therapist

_____

Group or individual _____

I talked to: (name) _____ (title) _____

$ per session _____

Available times to meet _____

Date of initial consultation _____

Individual Therapy

Make an appointment with one or two therapists, if you have that option, and ask for a consultation session so that you can see how you feel when you're with him or her. Ask yourself what feels right to you and what you feel uncomfortable about. Once you've taken this step, expect some resistance in yourself about going to your therapy session. Watch to see if you come up with reasons why you can't go. Many survivors have difficulty allowing themselves to choose the experiences and relationships they want to give themselves. Your therapist will become a very important person in your life, and will be one of your strongest allies in your recovery process. Give yourself the right to choose well.

> We begin life with the world presenting itself to us as it is. Someone—our parents, teachers, analysts—hypnotize us to "see" the world and construe it in the "right" way. These others label the world, attach names and give voices to the beings and events in it, so that thereafter we cannot read the world in any other language or hear it saying other things to us.
>
> The task is to break the hypnotic spell, so that we become undeaf, unblind, and multilingual, thereby letting the world speak to us in new voices and write all of its possible

meanings in the book of our existence. Be careful in your choice of hypnotists.

Sydney Jourard

Group Therapy

Therapy groups are different than the self-help groups listed in the "Community Organizations" section of this chapter in that they usually have a closed enrollment (meaning that the same members make a commitment to show up every time) and the maximum number of people is limited, typically to between four and twelve group members. Other therapy groups, however, may use an open "drop-in" format similar to self-help groups. In group therapy, the therapist usually takes a more active role in directing the group process than is the case in self-help groups, so it feels like someone is a little more "in charge."

The advantage of having the same members come every week is that it allows you to connect to a small, manageable number of people. You may begin to call each other during the week, or even develop friendships with group members that include social activities. These people may form the beginning of your recovery support system.

Initially, the most important task is to hear other women tell their stories, and watch and listen to them express their feelings. This goes a long way in normalizing your own healing process.

What Goes On? Examples of Different Types of Groups

Incest Survivor Process Groups or Therapy Groups

One therapist described the group's activities in the following way: "There is a lot of guilt work, and grieving and rage work. Survivors must grieve the losses, and there are many; the loss of a good family, of a mother to protect them, of a decent father, relationships with siblings, of their own experience of innocence; the list goes on and on. They must find ways to create a good new family and be their own good mother from within. In the anger work, a woman can beat on pillows with a plastic bat in the middle of the circle. Anybody can leave who needs to. There is a lot of talk about what they'd like to do to the offender at this stage. This is called the 'revenge fantasies' stage. Sometimes there is a lot of talk about how rotten the whole system is, which I usually block. I believe it's more important to stay with the feelings in a more personal way."

In **memory clarification groups**, members bring in pictures from childhood or pictures from each grade in school. Viewing old photographs depicting family members and childhood events can jar your memory of the incest experience, especially when you have only vague recollections of the past. Old photographs can bring memories of sexual abuse into sharper focus, making it more real and less like a dream or like something that happened to someone else.

Art therapy groups include such activities as having women make a collage of their life, including secret doors in the middle for the hidden part of their life. Brooke Passano, a therapist specializing in incest survivor recovery, says, "Sometimes writing poetry gets right to the feelings, or clay therapy can be a vehicle for expressing feelings trapped in the body that are not yet ready for words. Journal writing, either free-form or with suggested topics, is another good tool to start getting in touch with feelings and the inner self."

The following is an example of the way she works with groups:

> I focus on healing the inner "wounded child" and sometimes use creative visualization to help women get to know their own inner child. Since survivors have never known safety, I have them create in their imagination a safe place where they can start to get acquainted with their own inner child—perhaps a tree house, a play house, whatever comes to mind. It is not uncommon for survivors to be terrified of their own inner child.
>
> It is also useful to have the women observe a child the same age as they were when they were molested. Survivors tend to remember themselves as old and responsible. When they see the child they usually say, "She's so little." With compassion for the child, the healing begins.

61

Twelve Step Groups

The Twelve Steps of Alcoholics Anonymous were designed by two recovering alcoholics as a set of practical exercises to help alcoholics stay sober. Beginning with the admission of the need for help and the experience of surrendering to that need rather than fighting it, the steps continue to address central recovery issues. They allow individuals to clean up the past and develop a life that includes spirituality, meditation, and service. These principles form the blueprint for recovery for all the Twelve Step programs.

The Twelve Steps for Incest Survivors

The following is my version of the Twelve Steps adapted for incest survivors. They break through the denial, isolation, and feelings of shame, self-hate, and remorse to allow you to move on to a richer, fuller life and expression of yourself. This is strictly my interpretation and should not be construed as representing Incest Survivors Anonymous or any other Twelve Step group.

It is generally agreed that the steps are better worked with a sponsor, the person you select who has worked the steps herself and who can serve as a guide.

Each person's timetable to work through all Twelve Steps will be different. It is important to work the steps at your own pace, moving forward as you are ready and going back to rework past steps as necessary.

Step 1. We admitted we were powerless over the incest and that our lives had become unmanageable.

This step can help you break denial and admit there is a problem. Long-term residual effects of childhood sexual abuse can be disruptive to optimal functioning and give you a feeling that your life is unmanageable—"out of balance" or "off track." Admitting powerlessness and unmanageability does not mean defeat or self-blame. On the contrary, it's the first step in regaining power over your life. It's okay to take responsibility for your life and recovery without taking responsibility for the incest.

Keep in mind that as a child you needed your parents to survive. Whatever was done—including the incest—to preserve the connection was your attempt to thrive, not something to feel guilty about.

Step 2. We came to believe in a Power greater than ourselves that would restore us to sanity.

This is where many people get bogged down when trying out Twelve Step programs, because the terminology smacks of religious dogma, childhood memories of hand-slapping nuns, and visions of *One Flew over the Cuckoo's Nest*. However you are not confined to such "traditional" definitions of "Higher Power" or "sanity." Sanity in this case may be defined as a feeling of freedom and self-love; conversely, insanity can be thought of as denial, fear, or self-hate.

In order to take the first step of letting go and releasing the past, we must have something to hold on to, to satisfy the empty hole inside. A "power greater than ourselves" can be understood to mean a support group, a friend further along in recovery, or a therapist. (A word of caution: The last two are fine for right now, but not recommended for the long haul, because sooner or later one person will let you down.) It can mean a safe place that can ward off the terror, or a sense of connection with Universal Good, an order scheme, or Nature. It might be a soft voice inside you that provides loving instruction. Some people describe their Higher Power as a gut feeling that tells them when something is true.

There are as many different definitions of a Higher Power as there are people, and probably no organization in the world provides as much freedom to define your relationship with a Higher Power in your own individual way as do Twelve Step programs.

Step 3. We made a decision to turn our will and our lives over to the care of God as we understood Him.

It is unfortunate for incest survivors that the terminology uses "Him" rather than "It." The concept of turning one's life and will over to "Him" echoes past trauma. It's important to allow yourself to be creative and designate a Higher Power that is right for you. Some people find it helpful to think of the Higher Power as a Higher Self or as residing within themselves in a sacred place. Continue to substitute your own words—such as "Love," "Universal Goodness," "Good," "orderly direction," and so forth— whenever "God" is written in a step or when someone is speaking in a meeting.

The most important words in Step 3 are "care of"

because they may embody a concept that is new and foreign to an abuse survivor. You may have had no experience of anybody really caring about your needs and wants above their own. Caring also means loving, and you may need to experience unconditional love from other people before you can transfer that concept to an Unseen Being.

This is what makes Twelve Step programs different than other religious organizations—the emphasis is on honest, open relationships with other human beings and allowing spiritual help to come through people.

Step 3 is the beginning of trust and is not to be undertaken lightly by anyone who has had her trust as severely violated as an incest survivor has. However, surrender is essential to the Twelve Step philosophy because it permits the release of the ego so that you may gain entrance into the Higher Mind or Universal Consciousness. This is the point at which peak experiences and union with all that's good can occur. By letting go we can allow a greater power to do for us what is humanly impossible.

Step 4. We made a searching and fearless moral inventory of ourselves.

Inventory means taking stock of your assets and debits (deficiencies) so that you can discover what you have, what you want to keep, and what you want to discard.

Step 4 begins to change the habit of running away from looking at yourself, the habit of stuffing the feelings and going numb. It's the beginning of getting out some of the pain and shame you've been carrying around with you all your life. You are setting down some of your baggage on paper. In Step 5 you'll go further, giving it to another human being and your Higher Power so that you don't have to keep lugging around your past everywhere you go.

In this step you are asked to write an inventory of your experiences. While Twelve Step literature tends to focus this part of recovery on the idea of defects of character, this is a tricky business for a shame-based survivor struggling not to take on responsibility for her abuser's illness. A more useful focus for a survivor may be in taking this opportunity to look into yourself and tell the truth about your feelings. It can be a very freeing experience to slow down, stop running, and put some thoughts and images down on paper.

Never walk away from a writing session without something good. If you can't think of something good about yourself, read something spiritual and uplifting. (Emmett Fox's *Sermon on the Mount*, Shakti Gawain and Laurel King's *Living in the Light*, and Catherine Ponder's *The Dynamic Laws of Prosperity* are a few examples.)

It is important to know that writing Step 4 is an emotionally and spiritually vulnerable time. The very process of writing, or even becoming willing to write, can stir up a lot of old, painful memories, and sometimes thoughts about drinking or using drugs or hurting yourself start getting stronger. If you sense strong obsessions and compulsions, move back to Step 3 and rest there for a little while, but keep the energy moving if you can. You don't want to stagnate in your recovery.

The object of Step 4 is to puncture the defenses and remove blame. The inventory can be just a few pages or an autobiography. The important task is to open the door to the habit of reflection and introspection—to act in direct opposition to denial, the core of all shame-based, obsessive-compulsive diseases.

Step 5. We admitted to God, to ourselves, and to another human being the exact nature of our wrongs.

Nowhere is it more important than in incest survivor recovery for you to share your internal experience with another human being. A big part of the healing is in telling the story. After going through the process of writing your inventory in Step 4, it's very important to express and release the information, particularly if any of it has been held secret. Without Step 5, you may feel as if everything painful is all stirred up with no place to go, and this can be a period in recovery when obsession and compulsion return. The period between Steps 4 and 5 is a slippery time in sobriety. Don't sit on it. Think of Step 5 as washing away the old so there is room to let in some good. This is the beginning of taking healthy risks, learning to trust, and opening up to admit another person into your life.

Some people write Step 4 and share it with their sponsor, clergyman, friend, or spiritual mentor a section at a time, so it doesn't feel so overwhelming. It also is a good idea to have one person know your entire inventory. Important: If anything you're writing about makes you feel like drinking or using drugs, tell somebody right away.

Step 6. We were entirely ready to have God remove all these defects of character.

This step can be a huge relief because it tells us that we don't have to change all by ourselves. All we have to do is be willing to change and ask our Higher Power for help.

This step allows you to develop ongoing self-awareness. This can be an entirely new position of empowerment and freedom from old belief systems that have kept you locked in repetitive experiences. Steps 6 and 7 are particularly important in the development of relationships because as you start to get close to other people, it is inevitable that conflicts will arise. It is not uncommon for survivors to attract abusive relationships, simply from not having had a chance to develop *antennae* to see them coming.

The other common relationship pattern survivors fall into is to isolate themselves. For a person who hasn't yet learned how to choose healthy people for relationships, or yet developed the self-worth to sustain closeness, being able to be honest and take responsibility for 50 percent—rather than 100 percent —of current relationship problems is a way out of those destructive patterns.

Step 7. We humbly asked Him to remove our shortcomings.

This step is a wonderful reminder that there is a Higher Power operating in the universe that can aid us when we have reached our own or others' human limits. The abandonment wound that incest leaves is so huge that sometimes there is no other place to turn than to an unlimited Higher Power.

The goal here is to become a "True Self," free of defenses or behaviors that don't produce the results you want now. The message is that we are meant to be the best we can be and have the kind of life that we desire. It's hard to create that, to attract good experiences and relationships, when we're contracted with fear or pushing people away with unresolved resentments. Letting go of your defects allows the Higher Power to work more directly in your life. Synchronicity, magic, and miracles are part of the experiences that people report when their sense of "conscious contact" with their Higher Power increases.

Some people cling to their defects as a life preserver, as if they believe they will have no identity without them. The truth is that it's always more fun to be free of defects, for without them we can truly be free to be present in the current moment.

Step 8. We made a list of all persons we had harmed and became willing to make amends to them all.

Probably the first person to put on this list is yourself. Before attempting this step, it's a good idea to have a solid base of recovery, a good connection with some recovering people you can share questions with and get feedback from and a period of regular attendance at meetings. A survivor's tendency is to see the world through the perspective of "I'm wrong." Go gently with this; look through your life and see if there are any relationships where you feel incomplete. Write down your thoughts.

If there are any people or situations that make you cringe because of your own behavior, make a note of it, but definitely check out this list with your sponsor to insure that you're not beating yourself up or taking unnecessary responsibility for another person's defects. Because of their own lack of boundaries, many survivors feel accountable for other people's atrocious behavior.

It's not uncommon for people to be afraid of this step. It's important to remember you are only making a list at this point. Sometimes there's more pain incurred in avoiding people and life than in actually doing anything directly harmful to anyone.

Step 9. We made direct amends to such people whenever possible, except when to do so would injure them or others.

Keep in mind that you may be one of the "others" here. Again, it is advisable to go over your list with a sponsor or therapist before taking any action on it. It's very important not to put yourself in a situation that could hurt you. But if you've reviewed your list with someone and received their feedback on the advisability of contacting each person on your list, you are ready to proceed. Another idea is to use role play with a therapist or friend to anticipate how you will feel contacting someone on the list. If you do this and still feel the end result will be an improvement in your self-esteem, proceed.

Remember, making amends is for your benefit. A good indication of the appropriateness of your amends is that it doesn't matter to you what the other person's response will be, because you just want to do it for yourself.

I had the experience of making a very emotional call to a male family member to say, "I want to apologize for everything that's ever happened between us. I realize that I wrote you off as a human being and saw you as cold and remote. Now I realize that I shut down and withdrew from you and I'd like to not do that anymore."

His response was, "Oh, well, uh, how's your car running?"

The proof that it was time to make this call was that his response caused no pain. He was just being who he was.

The point of this step is to make us free. If possible, we need to say the words of our amends to the person on our list. Some of the people on the list may not be able to hear the amends—they may be dead, physically too far away, or emotionally inaccessible. In these cases, you can either write a letter to their Higher Self, or go through the process of saying the words out loud, in order to send them out on a spiritual level. If you do try to talk to someone directly and it doesn't appear that he has heard you—for example, if his eyes show no recognition—you can rest assured that he did hear you on some level of his being.

Step 10. We continued to take personal inventory and when we were wrong, promptly admitted it.

In addition to the freeing habit of being able to admit, "I made a mistake," this step can also take the form of promptly reporting your feelings in close relationships when the alternative is to shut down. Step

10 can help you say, "I don't understand why you just said or did that. I'm feeling confused . . . hurt, scared, angry." This is what healthy vulnerability and staying in love is all about. Vulnerability does not have to equal fragility; it can be a very powerful place from which to operate. It allows people in relationships to keep the channels open and to keep things clear, so that layers of resentment, hurt, and fear never have to pile up. It's much easier to work out misunderstandings as they occur than to struggle with those that have accumulated over time.

You may choose to do a written inventory every night, going over a list of such questions as, "Whom did I hurt?" "Where was I self-seeking?" "Where was I helpful?" "What good did I do today?" This step continues to reinforce the habit of honest self-appraisal, a necessary skill for building self-esteem and allowing emotional intimacy with others.

Step 11. We sought through prayer and meditation to improve our conscious contact with God, as we understood Him, praying only for the knowledge of His will for us and the power to carry that out.

This step implies the necessity of ongoing contact with one's spiritual source, to receive strength, hope, and guidance for life's day-to-day stresses. Developing the habit of "going inside" to gain clarity and balance allows us to take better care of the "small voice" that possesses a higher wisdom than our ordinary mind, especially when we're frazzled. Doing nothing but spending ten to twenty minutes in prayer, meditation, or contemplation every day over a period of time can produce a change in perspective that gradually changes one's character so that you become a gentler, kinder, more genuine, and more powerful person.

Some techniques that people find helpful to induce a contemplative state include listening to music or repeating again and again such phrases as, "I am Love, I am Light, I am Beauty, I am Power"; "Peace is filling me now"; or "I am a radiant child of God."

Step 12. Having had a spiritual awakening as a result of these Steps, we tried to carry this message to others and to practice these principles in all our affairs.

This step provides hope that there will be a new feeling about life and that healing is possible. Once this awakening is experienced, there will be a natural interest in and outflow to others. This interest may begin with a desire to help other addicts and/or survivors and then gradually be extended to safe family members, the community, and then to social or political causes. A valuable slogan at this point is, "We've got to give it away to keep it." It also underlies the importance of having a faith that we can bring into our everyday lives, and an ability to apply our principles to live our lives with compassion and order.

AMELIA'S STORY

Introduction

Amelia's story is presented here because it contains some good insights on how to choose a therapist and the kinds of qualities and considerations one may find important in a therapist. It is also a good example of a survivor's experiences as her childhood amnesia begins to thaw.

Amelia is a single, white, lesbian woman in her mid-twenties. The youngest of three children by eight years, Amelia has always had a sense of separateness. Her mother was a prescription drug addict and a compulsive overeater; it was Amelia's role to take care of her. Amelia describes her father as a "workaholic."

The perpetrator for Amelia was her older brother. Her memories of the molestation are vague and sometimes veiled in the language of her dreams or reactions to hearing other women's stories of being molested. There were always a variety of adults present in her household, and Amelia wonders if she was also molested by her brother-in-law, who was an alcoholic. There seem to have been very few generational boundaries in the family.

As a child, Amelia believed she was ugly and fat, and felt impaired socially. She began to abuse food as a child, and drugs and alcohol as a teenager. Like her mother, Amelia was depressed and suicidal. Her drugs of choice were prescription, primarily Percodan, which she received for "headaches." At the same time she was using drugs, Amelia was very active in extracurricular activities in high school ("anything so I didn't have to go home"). She attended a boarding school, studied compulsively, and always had excellent grades.

Amelia came out as a lesbian in high school but was not sexually active until her twenties. In one of her first serious relationships, she was confronted with her abuse of chemicals and began recovery three and a half years ago. At this time, her feelings about the incest intensified, and she began to attend Incest Survivors Anonymous. (This is a common pattern for many survivors, and will be examined in greater depth in Chapter Three.)

Amelia's story shares several elements with Grace's: Like Grace, Amelia was an amnesiac survivor, whose memories of the molestation emerged much later during hypnosis with her therapist. She continues to gather information about her abuse through various means, such as noticing her reactions to different stimuli. The effects of the overt incest were compounded by covert incest—her mother's emotional dependence on her daughter. As a result, Amelia's childhood, adolescence, and early adulthood were scarred by symptoms of Post-traumatic Stress Disorder, many of which she continues to deal with on a daily basis: poor self-esteem, anxiety, physical ailments, suicidal tendencies, and chemical dependency.

Recently, Amelia has worked professionally with survivors as a counselor and has been active as a public speaker on the subject. Her views on the choice of a therapist represent those of many survivors. However, many other survivors have very different viewpoints. You will need to make your own decisions, but it may be helpful to listen to her evaluations.

Amelia's Story

The perpetrator in my family was my brother, who was fourteen years older than me. I don't have clear memories. My best guess is that the incest occurred when I was about six or seven. I think there were other perpetrators, maybe my brother-in-law, maybe my mother. I'm not sure, probably some of my sisters' boyfriends; there were a lot of alcoholics and people around the house. There weren't any boundaries in the family. The abuse didn't end with my brother until he got married.

I had total memory loss of my childhood until about three years ago. The first time I had a memory was during a therapy session when I was being hypno- tized. We weren't trying to remember incest; it was accidental. I'd been in therapy for three and a half years at that time. When the memory surfaced, my therapist didn't deal with it well. She ignored it. I've since gone to Incest Survivors Anonymous.

Now I'll usually have a memory come up and then forget it. I'll have pictures, mostly still pictures. I've realized that sometimes I accidentally hurt myself be- fore I have a memory, drop things on my foot or burn myself, and that a lot of things I do are unconsciously designed to keep memories away. Sometimes mem- ories come more readily when I'm not in a conscious state. They seem to filter through in dreams or when I'm half awake—half asleep. Sometimes I'll see some- thing that reminds me of what I was like when I see a child, for instance, or I'll hear somebody else talking about something related to being molested and it'll sound very familiar. I don't have a lot of concrete memories, but I've had some.

My mom is a compulsive overeater; she has several eating disorders and uses prescription drugs, mostly amphetamines and diet pills. She was suicidal most of my life; although she didn't make any real attempts, she was always threatening to kill herself. I was put in the middle a lot with my mom and her eating disorders. I wanted her to go to a therapist, but she said, "I don't need one, I have you." She'd get hysterical and threaten suicide, and I took care of her.

In school I got straight As. I was always the teacher's pet. None of the kids ever liked me. Usually I'd have one best friend, but I was always terrified she would leave. I never felt secure. I didn't play with kids my own age much; I was always with kids who were older. But I always got As, and I was always in plays and musicals—anything I could be in after school to not have to go home.

I used to threaten to run away. I cut my wrists once, not seriously, but it was definitely a gesture. I considered a lot of things: overdosing, drowning myself. I felt suicidal often throughout my adolescence. I had seen my mom do that all my life; I thought it was normal. As a teenager I starved myself and cut myself. I hurt myself accidentally. When I was in my first relationship I would drive my car real crazy and cut myself with knives.

I've never really felt stable, and I have a lot of anxiety. I had no connection with my body and started abusing food real early. I started smoking pot at age ten or eleven. My mom told me to smoke at my sister's if I was going to do it. My sister was married to an alcoholic and there were always parties at their house. I didn't drink much but did acid and coke in high school. Then I started getting migraine headaches. I went to a military hospital, and they gave me these huge bottles of Percodan. When it got really bad they'd give me a shot of Demerol. So I got a lot of headaches. I had a friend whose father was a doctor and she'd get Valium from him. In college, I did more coke and pot and less acid.

I don't remember much about my childhood except the feeling that I was ugly and bad, as if I couldn't do anything right. I also had a lot of the issues I'm dealing with in relationships now: that I'm either too seductive and provocative or nothing, either I'm too sexual or not enough. I wasn't very sexual in high school. I came out as a lesbian, but I didn't really have relationships besides crushes. I've always been pretty shy, actually terrified about my body. I've always felt nobody would want to be sexual with me or be attracted to me; that's played a big part in most of my relationships. I think I used drugs a lot in order to feel okay about it.

In the last couple years I've been more sexual with more people. Two of the people I was involved with were incest survivors, and we'd talk a lot about and deal with it. The last woman I was involved with had flashbacks a lot. Sometimes it would bring up vague memories in me. Another time I was involved with somebody and we were just joking around. She said, "Oh, I know about girls like you," and I lost it. I had some sort of flashback that I don't remember now. What that comment set off in me was, "People only want to be around me for sexual reasons. That's all I'm good for and I caused it."

Other memories were triggered when I was with a

girlfriend who got violent a couple times. The first time that happened I had a strong reaction. I had always thought that I'd never been hit, but when I hear fights I always have a real strong reaction. I also noticed that when I get dressed up and go out sometimes I dress pretty provocatively. I get a lot of attention and, even though that's what I want, I disconnect from the part of me that likes it and I get uncomfortable with it.

I'm still dealing with migraines, back pain, and a lot of stress-related symptoms. I also have had some weird illnesses and symptoms that doctors can never locate.

I'm just beginning to deal with intimacy. I think I separate sex and intimacy, but I'm learning. I like it when I can put them together, but it scares me. I'm working on making choices—knowing that I have a choice about who I want to be intimate with, choosing people and times when I want to be intimate. I tend to do one of two things: I trust too much or I don't trust at all. I sometimes wonder what I would have been like without the incest. I'm sure it's affected me in being able to be close to people; I know it's affected my body image, my sense of self; that's probably the major way.

In therapy, I think it's important for survivors to work with women, even if the perpetrator wasn't a man. I just don't believe men can deal with this. I'm not sure that strict psychoanalytic therapy is useful because survivors need to have a little more intimacy. It's also good to have something other than just talking, like exercises and homework. A therapist should have a nice room, a safe-looking space, and unconditional belief in what the client says. For groups, it might be important for the therapist to be an incest survivor because survivors need to have role models who are doing well. Therapists should have knowledge about substance abuse, since almost all the survivors I've seen have had some history of substance abuse. It's necessary to have a real strict agreement about not using and drinking while people are dealing with this. And I don't think short-term therapy works.

One mistake I think therapists can make is to focus on the incest experience as being part of the choice to be lesbian. I've heard some real horror stories about that. Therapists need to know there's no cause and effect in these issues. *Lesbian Passion*, by JoAnn Loulan, is a lesbian book that has a really good chapter on incest. She suggests that you get in touch with your child by getting a lifelike doll. When you're feeling vulnerable, you can care for the doll. She goes on to suggest that you give the doll a separate place in your house, maybe in the closet, so the doll's got its own space, for you to get in touch with the feeling of being taken care of.

Your notes on Amelia's Story:

What do you identify with in Amelia's story? Make a note of anything you found disturbing or that stimulated any memories.

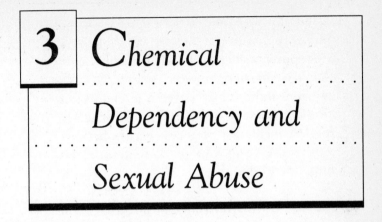

3 Chemical
Dependency and
Sexual Abuse

If you are an addict, an alcoholic, and/or ACA as well as an incest survivor, you have a unique healing journey. This chapter is designed to address the special issues you face in your recovery and to let you know what to expect.

No discussion of incest survivor recovery is complete without looking at the strong connection between chemical dependency and incest abuse. Claudia Black, an internationally known therapist and speaker on ACA recovery and author of *It Will Never Happen to Me*, states:

> Twenty-five million children under the age of eleven have been sexually abused. . . . While research concerning incest and its relationship to alcohol and abuse is limited and varies in its conclusions, a number of studies document that over 50 percent of known incest

victims live in homes where there is alcohol abuse. In addition, many private practitioners report 60–80 percent of alcoholic women they treat were once incest victims. My own research indicates 26 percent of children in alcoholic homes have been incest victims. The highest incidence of incest occurs between adult fathers and younger daughters or stepfathers and daughters.

Stephanie Covington states in a study on the differences in sexual abuse experienced by alcoholic and nonalcoholic women, "Incest accounted for 34% of the reported sexual abuse among the [alcoholic] subjects, or double that for the nonalcoholic population, of whom 16 percent had experienced sexual abuse involving incest." Covington also found that 14 percent of the alcoholic women reported sexual abuse by the same perpetrator over a period of ten years or longer, while none of the nonalcoholic subjects reported abuse over so long a period.

Most incest survivors come from "polyabusive" homes in which substance abuse, physical abuse, and sexual abuse coexist. The number of women who have multiple chemical dependency, ACA, and incest survivor issues has not been calculated, but the cycle is easy to see.

Parents under the influence of chemicals and whose lives are focused around drinking or using drugs are incapable of attending to their children's needs or separating their personal needs from their children's. This lack of generational and personal boundaries, combined with alcohol's effect of lowering inhibitions, can increase the likelihood of a parent acting out sexually.

Many times the sexual abuse occurs during an alcoholic "black-out." Black-outs are defined as periods when the alcohol in the blood reaches such a level that the brain stops recording events. Different than passing out, black-outs can last hours or even years, during which the alcoholic appears to be functioning normally. It is not unusual for an alcoholic to engage in sexual activity during a black-out and afterward have absolutely no memory of it. Events that occur during black-outs cannot be recalled because they were never recorded by the brain. This can be particularly disturbing and confusing if a survivor attempts to confront the abuser later without being able to validate the abuse.

Chemical dependency also contributes to sexual abuse of children when co-parents (the other, "non-abusive" parent) neglect to observe or blatantly deny the evidence of the abuse. Many cases in which the child's distress signals are "not seen" or responded to by the co-parent may be attributed to a parent's own addiction or ACA issues.

As they mature, it is not uncommon for survivors to begin to abuse substances themselves. Often by preadolescence (ten to twelve years old) they are into their own "full-blown" addiction in an effort to kill the pain. In recovery, these "coping skills" must be unlearned and new skills substituted that allow the pain to surface to tolerable levels.

GETTING CLEAN AND SOBER

If you are already clean and sober, you may still want to read through this section. Since many survivor issues are so interrelated, there may be much to interest you, too.

If you are an incest survivor and an alcoholic or addict, your first priority must be abstinence from all mood-changing substances. You can't do anything about incest survivor recovery if you're drunk or high. Only when the using and drinking behavior is stabilized is it possible to begin the in-depth work of exploring feelings and relationship difficulties. It is also appropriate then to look at childhood trauma, including the incest, and how it is interfering with current relationships, goals, and dreams.

If you are not sure whether you're an addict or an alcoholic, you might want to try staying abstinent for a time, just to clean out your body and to allow whatever emotions you may be anesthetizing to reveal themselves. Choose a specific length of time to be drug or alcohol free: a week, a month, ninety days. Share this agreement with someone you can check in with and report how it's going. A good measurement for deciding how long your abstinence should be is to think back on how long it's been since you've been completely drug and alcohol free for any length of time.

Once you've started your abstinence, notice all your thoughts and feelings about not drinking or using. Do you feel deprived? Relieved? Euphoric? Confused, or as if there's something missing? Does your mind come up with rationalizations about why you don't really have to stop, or why it's okay to have "just one" or to indulge "just this time"? Are you comparing yourself to those other "poor people" who "really have a problem"? When attempting to define whether you have a problem with chemical dependency, you must always be aware of tendencies toward rationalization, justification, intellectualization, and denial. These are all different ways your mind protects you from honestly looking at yourself. This is why it's so necessary to have another person involved in your agreement to abstain. If you unconsciously start to change the rules, you'll have a reminder of the original agreement.

If you have trouble keeping your agreement with yourself about not using any mood-changing substances for a specific period of time, this may be evidence that you are powerless over them. It may mean that you've crossed that line between social drinking or using and addictive use.

First, therefore, you need to learn how not to pick up the drink or drug. That is Step 1 of the Twelve Steps: "We admitted we were powerless over alcohol/drugs and that our lives had become unmanageable." This usually requires a support group who understands obsession and compulsion and the insanity of using over and over again, even when you've decided you don't want to do it anymore. This is what is referred to as powerlessness. If you can't have just one drink or drug, or if, once you've had one, you can't predict where it will end, you don't have power over the substance. It is controlling you. If you can see that drugs or alcohol are making your life unmanageable—meaning you find yourself doing crazy things, feeling remorseful after using, or not living up to your own expectations because your use is interfering with your intentions—you need help. You need to be with some people who have lived through the same problem and have made it to the other side. They are the best teachers about how to get and stay clean and sober because they understand not only the mechanics of it but also the feelings involved.

Every one of us has the right to make his or her own decisions about defining ourselves as an addict or alcoholic, and gaining the support that feels right for us. If you decide you do want or need to get clean and sober, the first requirement is learning what behavior and thinking sets off your obsessions (repetitive, intrusive thinking about your drug of choice) and compulsions (behavior that feels out of control). The next step is learning what thinking and behavior to substitute for the self-destructive patterns. This usually requires group support because the need is so strong. The highest success rate for chemical dependency recovery is through Alcoholics Anonymous and Narcotics Anonymous. This is because the dependency on the substances has to be transferred to a healthy dependency on other people and also to a spiritual source. The Twelve Steps lead you step by step through this process. See Chapter Two for more information.

STAGE I RECOVERY

There are predictable developmental stages to recovery from chemical dependency. Knowing what to expect of yourself and what you need can make the difference between successfully maintaining sobriety or having a relapse. These stages are outlined in Earnie Larsen's *Stage II Recovery* and Stephanie Brown's *A Developmental Model of Recovery*. Larson defines Stage I as the prerequisite breaking of the primary addiction. Brown notes that this stage is a matter of behavioral and cognitive change: learning how not to drink or use. Stage II broadens the focus of recovery to include emotional, spiritual, and relationship issues.

In Stage I you will need to concentrate on the reality that alcohol and drugs will not solve life's problems, or even reduce the pain. They will only make things worse. If you started your recovery focusing on the incest and then decided to get drug or alcohol free, you may find fewer memory and feeling releases during the first few months of sobriety. When you realize how much of your past life was spent thinking about, planning, and anticipating using or drinking, it makes sense that it will take some time to "reprogram" your thoughts. Repeating AA/NA slogans and language helps to reinforce the cognitive (mental) changes taking place. Repetition is one of the best forms of internalizing new information.

People don't separate from something they've loved in one day, and you may experience an internal conflict about wanting to drink or use drugs for some time. To defend against this, you may go through a period of needing to be rigid about not tolerating anything that could pull you back into the vulnerability of wanting to drink or use. You may need to change the people you see and spend time with, where you live, where you work, where you go for relaxation, what you do for fun, what you talk about, read, watch on TV, which commercials you see or what music you hear.

This is the time to replace old coping skills with new ones. Again, Twelve Step programs can help you find behaviors that encourage abstinence and provide you with the beginnings of the strong support system you will need. New behaviors include attending meetings, reading Twelve Step literature and slogans, making phone calls to AA/NA members, making commitments to prepare coffee at meetings, and so forth. These activities replace the old drinking and using behaviors and represent a shift from an addictive lifestyle to a clean and sober lifestyle.

For the chemically dependent/ACA/incest survivor, it is important not to take on too much in the first year of sobriety, so that you may stabilize new non-addictive behaviors. However, repressed pain sometimes makes its way to the surface; if not released, this pain can create enough discomfort to threaten sobriety and make a relapse appear preferable.

It takes some difficult balancing, then, to acknowledge some of the feelings and relieve some of the pressure and, at the same time, to learn to back off if you begin to feel flooded. Some recovering addicts and survivors find they need to "put a lid" on their sexual abuse issues and buy some time just to concentrate on abstinence and to build up their support systems. It is probably not a good idea to get too far into uncovering memories before you've developed at least the capacity to pick up the phone and reach out to someone when you're hurting.

Phone resources may be the most important coping skill for the sexual abuse survivor, because the intensity of the feelings can be so great and unpredictable. These feelings are a terrifying prospect for all recovering people, but if she experiences shame from childhood abuse experiences, a survivor may find this to be a particularly formidable task.

If you feel you are incapable of calling someone when you're hurting, you should probably be in therapy, so that you will be forced to work directly on building trust. In the meantime, see if you can guide yourself slowly and gently through your fear. However terrifying, at some point it is essential to take a deep breath, ask yourself, "What lengths am I willing to go to for my recovery?" and pick up the phone. Even if you're shaking, you can get through it. It may take you a few trials of picking up the phone and hanging up while it's ringing, but keep going. Hang in there. It does get easier.

During Stage I there is sometimes a period of euphoria called the "pink cloud" stage. It is not uncommon for this initial stage to be followed by a period of irritation and restlessness and a feeling that "something is missing." This is an indication that it is time to move on to the deeper level of growth in Stage II.

STAGE II RECOVERY

The only true cure for addiction is replacing the chemical dependency cravings with healthy intimate relationships. Without the chemicals, the old, painful abandonment wounds surface; without the anesthesia the chemicals provide, the pain can be too overwhelming to bear. This causes a flare-up of drug and alcohol cravings or a switch to other compulsive behavior such as eating disorders or compulsive sex, spending, work, or gambling. If we don't go forward, we go backward.

Trust is an essential component of recovery. A person in recovery cannot continue in isolation; relapse is inevitable. It is not enough to simply learn skills of how not to pick up a drink or a drug, one day at a time, as important as that is as the first step. The next step requires opening the door to ACA or family-of-origin issues.

Sharing and communicating "what's going on now" with other recovering addicts and co-dependents is a life-and-death issue. The dilemma for the chemically dependent person raised in an alcoholic or sexually abusive home is that you have few relationship or communication skills. The typical ACA/incest family system contains the injunctions "Don't talk. Don't trust. Don't feel."

John Bradshaw defines dysfunctional families as those that produce "toxic shame" in children. The incest survivor is the most shame-based of all abused children. It is very difficult to ask for help when one is ashamed of the need for it, or is vacillating in and out of denial to anesthetize the pain of the wound.

As a recovering addict/ACA/incest survivor you are in a terrible bind if you are unable to face the underlying feelings and early-life traumas. You will need to restructure your earlier abusive experiences through therapy or other internal work. The following process exercise will help you get started. This restructuring will be discussed further in chapters Four and Five on grieving and raging and Inner Child work. Without doing your emotional clearing work and learning how to be more nurturing to yourself, you are in danger of recreating some form of abuse in your new relationships. Incest survivors often unconsciously select relationships with people who will be abandoning or verbally and/or physically abusive, even in NA and AA. This can create so much anxiety and shame that it becomes difficult for you to open up to members of your AA, NA, or ACA group.

PROCESS FOR CONTACTING FEELINGS

If you have difficulty identifying or knowing what words describe feelings, look over the following list to see if reading these words resonates with something inside you.

If you're aware of any feelings as a result of reading this list of questions, write them down now.

If you're not in the habit of knowing how to identify your feelings, copy this list down on a 3 × 5 card. Carry the card around with you for a week and, whenever a situation occurs that makes you feel uncomfortable, pull it out and read through the list again. See if you can begin to differentiate between these different feeling states.

ashamed	observed
afraid	lost
annoyed	abandoned
anxious	suffocated
angry	overwhelmed
irritated	hurt
guilty	left out
lonely	confused
sad	caved in
jealous	envious
terrified	responsible
self-conscious	disconnected
embarrassed	numb
pained	hyper/speedy
curious	unloveable
startled	repulsive
disappointed	peaceful
disoriented	calm
disbelieving	loving
shocked	understood
"seen through"/	
penetrated	

Particularly if you usually react to all events with one feeling state, such as anger, take some time and see if you have some other feelings that the anger is covering. Is there some sadness or disappointment going on in you as well? The same thing is usually true with depression— are you perhaps also angry? Boredom is another good "catch-all" feeling description that usually masks another feeling, such as frustration or anger at yourself.

PROCESSES FOR OBSESSIVE-COMPULSIVE BEHAVIOR

The process of recovery from any obsessive-compulsive disorder is learning how to track the thoughts and feelings precipitating the obsession. Obsession is a repetitive, intrusive thought you can't shake. Obsessions are usually followed by compulsive behavior. If you think about something long enough, you'll find your body doing it. It sometimes feels as if the activity isn't connected to you, as if your body has a will of its own. People report "finding" themselves with a drink in their hand, or in the midst of any number of other self-destructive activities. Recovery is increasing your awareness of everything that led up to the self-destructive impulse and learning to be sensitive enough to your own patterns that you can eliminate and protect yourself from your triggers.

When you recognize a trigger, the important task is learning how to derail the obsessive thought. Like a train going downhill, the more self-destructive thoughts you allow yourself to hold onto, the more powerful they will get. How can you interrupt it? What can you substitute for it?

Ask yourself the following questions and start to observe yourself over time:

Do you know what you were feeling right before you had a compulsion to self-mutilate or do anything self-destructive?

What were you thinking about?

For how long? Did the thoughts come on all at once or creep in slowly with increasing intensity?

Can you ask another person to help you with this?

When you feel drawn to act on a compulsion, call someone. Read something. Repeat a comforting thought to block it out. AA has some great slogans designed for this purpose, such as "Easy does it," "One day at a time," "Live and let live," "Think it through," and the Serenity Prayer: "God, Grant me the serenity to accept the things I cannot change, the courage to change the things I can, and the wisdom to know the difference."

Say these slogans over and over to yourself to block out the self-destructive thoughts. You can only think one thought at a time and only you can choose which thoughts you're going to entertain. Twelve Step programs have a great philosophy about this when they say, "You're not responsible for the first thought, only for what you do about it."

Other phrases to use for thought substitution are: "I am Love," "I am Peace," "I am One with all Good," "I am Divinely guided and protected at all times," and "Peace is filling me now."

COURTNEY'S STORY

Introduction

The following story powerfully illustrates the ways in which the dynamics of being an addict, an ACA, and an incest survivor interact with one another, and identifies some of the difficulties this woman has experienced in juggling these recovery processes.

Courtney is a thirty-four-year-old single, white, gay-identified woman. She is very pretty, with an incongruently apologetic, self-effacing style. Her parents, both alcoholics, were sexually abused as children. As parents they were abusive and neglectful. Courtney's father molested his stepson, Courtney's half-brother, between the ages of eight and twelve. Courtney's first molestation by her half-brother occurred when she was three years old, and she remembers feeling ashamed and bad from that time on.

Her early abuse left Courtney unable to process the losses incurred with her parents' divorce when she was thirteen. During this time of vulnerability, Courtney suffered more trauma from five years of sexual abuse by her stepfather. From the age of twenty until she achieved sobriety five years later, Courtney was addicted to heroin and alcohol, and abused cocaine.

Courtney's experiences reflect many of the themes and patterns common to addict/ACA/incest survivors. Because her early development was interrupted by multiple traumas and abandonments, her recovery must include the stages of growth that she missed. For incest survivors, the first of these is almost always learning how to trust, both in other human beings and in oneself.

All children need to have some healthy experience of bonding before they can set out into the world and develop the ability to care for themselves. Most survivors feel a lot of confusion about what constitutes self-care and how to have healthy boundaries. This is reflected in Courtney's relationship with her step-father, an alcoholic who physically abused her.

Courtney's competition with her mother for her stepfather's attention is a good illustration of en-meshment, the lack of boundaries or differentiation between the self and another. Courtney's experience is that she is either left totally alone and abandoned, or she is connected to her mother as an undifferen-tiated mass. This enmeshment continued into adult-hood as Courtney and her mother used drugs and drank together.

Courtney's first task in recovery was breaking denial about her addiction. Like many addicts, Courtney found this a difficult transition, requiring more than one attempt. The NA community, however, was avail-able when she needed it. As she began her recovery from chemicals, Courtney was able to concentrate on getting clean and sober. The incest issues did not be-gin again for her until two to three years after her sobriety. Then, she reports, the feelings were so over-whelming that she relapsed to drinking, until she rec-ognized the need to "open up" and let others in. This was the turning point. Ready now to deal with the several issues in her life as an ACA/addict/survivor, Courtney continues to work on all issues and feels she is making progress, although it is not easy. She must still work on coming to terms with her family of origin and on expressing anger.

Courtney's Story

My first molestation occurred when I was three years old. My half-brother, who was ten at the time, asked me to come into his room to tickle him, then pushed my hand down toward his penis and ejaculated. I felt embarrassed and humiliated. I tried to make like it was okay and laughed to cover it up. My response was to tell no one, to not think about it, and "stuff the feelings."

The second incidence occurred when I was eleven years old, when the same half-brother came into my room at night. I pretended I was asleep. He touched my leg from the bottom on up. When he got near my genitals I made a noise and he left. He might have gotten on top of my covers, but I moved around like I was going to wake up and he ran out of the room. This occurred about four times over the next three years. He would do it to my friends when they would spend the night. He also made a pass at my mother.

My step-grandfather (who had abused my mother) would bounce me on his lap with a hard-on. I'd ask him to stop it and he'd laugh. I felt dirty, humiliated, like a piece of crap.

Then my parents divorced when I was thirteen.

With my family broken up, I felt like I wanted to take care of my mother and my father. I especially felt sorry for my dad. I tried to be strong, but I really needed love. I didn't get it from my parents, so I grabbed it from my mother's boyfriend. He took advantage of the situation. When he first kissed me with his tongue, I ran away. Then I decided I wanted it and that I would do whatever he wanted.

I don't really remember being with K—it's fuzzy. We did everything, oral sex and everything you could imagine. I thought I was totally in love with him and he was totally in love with me. When we were together I felt okay, until I had to go home and deal with what was really happening. I was scared to death that I had to lie, and remember and keep track of all my lies. I felt desperate, black, just dark. I was all alone, I didn't have my family, my mother, my father, or anybody.

I felt guilty that I was taking my mother's boyfriend away. Then they got married and after a while it was even worse. I was already feeling broken up and vulnerable, but now I was in competition with my mother. She often called me a slut, but I might have felt like one even if she hadn't. I felt dirty even before K.

My mom and K would be making love after he and I had made love, or whatever you call it. I remember listening to it and crying and being confused and trying not to cry because I couldn't let my mom see.

I cut school a lot to be with K. My brother was home a couple of times when K and I made it, and my brother blamed me and hated me. There were many fights, and K moved out and came back. Once after a big fight I hid in the backseat of K's car before he got into it and then popped up after a block or so as he was driving away.

I went to stay with him in his duplex. That might have been the first night we had intercourse. My dad came looking for me, he knocked and knocked and then left. I remember feeling terrified. I was making a choice between my parents and K, and I felt real bad about it. But my parents didn't want me anyway, or that's what I thought. Then the police came, and we had to be real quiet.

The next day I went to school and they caught me. My mother came down and, in front of all my peers, said, "Was his dick good?" and shit like that. It was really embarrassing. She went wild and started hitting me.

I asked to go to Juvenile Hall so they took me there. Now I didn't have K or my family; I had nobody. I stayed there for three days. Then my mom felt sorry for me and got me out. When I saw her I knew she loved me, but I felt like I wasn't her daughter anymore. I was another woman. I felt worthless and hopeless. I just let her hit me; I yelled back, too, but part of me felt like I deserved to get hit.

When we got home, my mom called my dad over and made sure K was there. My dad beat the hell out of him. I just stood there and saw the insanity of it all. I didn't know who to side with, so I just went blank.

After high school I went to live with K and his mother. They were both alcoholics and were drunk all the time. I would cry and he'd hit me. Once I got real angry and went to get a gun. I was never going to shoot it, but that was pretty much the end.

Two years later I was addicted to heroin. My very

last contact with K was when I needed money. I got all dressed up to go down to the sleazy hotel where he was living at that point. Basically I was going to whore myself for some money. He touched my behind and I felt nothing. The drugs always help you feel nothing. If I did feel anything, it was disgust. I was surprised at that because I was so much in love with him for so long.

As a teenager, I had experimented with drugs a little bit but I had never really gotten into them. When I was a kid I always told myself I would never drink because I didn't want to be like my parents. When I was fourteen I drank a little but didn't like the taste. I experimented with pot, cross-tops, and acid, but I didn't get into it. Then at nineteen, I became a heavy user. When I did cocaine, something took over and I felt addictive about it immediately. By twenty I was physically addicted to heroin and alcohol, and had a strong psychological addiction to coke. I drank a lot to come down from the coke. That lasted until I was twenty-five.

I believe the reason I used drugs was I couldn't deal with the feelings and pain from the past. I also believe I have an addictive personality and if I hadn't used drugs it would have been something else: food, money, whatever could take the feelings away.

I was feeling suicidal and something inside was telling me there's got to be another way. I was working at a shop at the time and was always getting in trouble for my irresponsibility and making mistakes. I broke down and thought I was going crazy. I saw a psychiatrist very briefly, and he told me he couldn't see me unless I dealt with my addiction. He told me about Narcotics Anonymous meetings.

The first time I went to an NA meeting, I knew it was the place for me. I listened as well as I possibly could. These people were talking about the way I felt. For years I thought I was the only one who felt that way. I heard hopeful messages and for some reason I believed them. It didn't stop my using right away. I was in and out of the program for a while because I was in so much denial.

Then I moved in with my mother, and everything got totally insane. We were using together and the feelings were getting worse and worse. I took a handful of pills in a suicide attempt, and my mom took me to the crisis unit. From there I got into a recovery home.

In early sobriety I learned a lot. I even cried and talked about my stepfather, but the feelings didn't connect. I didn't have to deal with too many feelings about the incest in the beginning. I believe my Higher Power made it easy for me not to have to concentrate on both.

Once I got sober, sex repulsed me. The first time I had sex in sobriety, I cried the whole time and then felt disgusted. At first I thought I was crying for all the times I'd felt like a whore in my addiction.

At about two to three years clean and sober, the incest issues really began to surface and I started to hit an emotional bottom. I was in a relationship with a woman who was emotionally available to me when the incest issues came up, and I couldn't handle it. She wanted to have sex with me and be there for me. I totally shut down to her and was disgusted by sex.

Somebody told me about the symptoms of incest and suggested that what I was going through might be linked to it. That's how I got into the Incest Survivor treatment group. I knew immediately it was home. I've continued to work on the incest issues ever since.

I've been through many different phases in my recovery. Basically it's been pretty hard. I do have moments of calmness and joy more now than I ever have in the past five years. But most of my recovery has been more painful than anything else. The feelings got so heavy when I started to delve into the incest; it was overwhelming and I didn't trust myself to sit through it. It was so scary. I felt guilty, suicidal, and like destroying myself. It was about this time that I relapsed and drank again. I decided I had to do more work than I'd been willing to do before if I was going to make it.

So, in addition to going to the Incest Survivor Recovery group, I started seeing a therapist regularly, going to ACA and Al-Anon, and then I started to feel better. I realized I have several issues to deal with and I have to keep working on all of them. I need to work the Twelve Steps as well as deal with my feelings and incest memories.

Prior to this, I had gotten to a point where I didn't feel comfortable in NA and AA anymore. I wanted to talk about my feelings and what was going on right then, and nobody seemed to be talking about that. I had no interest in the past; I could care less about talking about using.

After I had the relapse, the feelings were so intense

I cried harder than I ever have in my life, and I had to let people in. I don't know exactly what it meant, but I think I was finally bringing the pain from the past into all my relationships. I was finally forced to share it with people. Luckily that last relapse turned out to be a turning point. It was very painful at the time, but it helped me to open up.

At this point in my recovery, I'm starting to have moments of euphoria. The other day I could even say out loud that I'm happy. But right away I started sabotaging it. I wasn't aware at the time, but in hindsight I see that I felt I didn't deserve it. I'm not used to it. I don't know how to handle it. I sabotage myself by self-mutilation, picking my eyelashes. After I do it I'm in so much agony trying to hide the fact that I have no eyelashes and putting makeup on to camouflage the way I've been picking my face. If I'm driving and can't get to my eyelashes, I start putting myself down mentally, until I'm panicking. It's like I still feel guilty and I'm trying to hurt myself. If anybody around me ever feels threatened, I'll downplay myself. At times I do enjoy being attractive, but it hits a point and I can't handle it anymore. All this is due to a lack of love. I don't love myself, but I'm learning how.

I was violated and abused and I carry that with me today. I don't know about healthy sex because the incest left such a scar on me that even if I had a healthy partner making love to me, I wouldn't know it, because I still feel like that kid. Ninety-five percent of the time, I've had sex for the other person. I've faked orgasm to please them. The thought of going on a date right now repulses me. But one day, I'll be able to be healthy and have healthy sex.

It took me a few years of sobriety to be ready to deal with the incest. At this point I look forward to going to my Incest Survivor group except for when I feel like I'm at a plateau with no new revelations. I know that until I process the incest issues, whatever it takes, I'm going to always be affected by the incest for the rest of my life. I have to know that it wasn't my fault and learn how to feel good about myself, which I never did; I never knew how to. Then I'll know I have rights, that I can take care of myself, and say no or say yes.

I feel that incest survivor treatment is the safest place, even more safe than when I got into Narcotics Anonymous. I mean, this is a whole other thing. This is the core, this is why I used drugs and alcohol.

I'm suffering for the incest today on a daily basis even though it happened years and years ago. Many days I feel like I'm fourteen, going through all the same feelings as I did then, waking up, feeling totally desperate, thinking, "I can't do it. How am I going to make it? How am I going to get through the day?" I'm really sick of it. I get angry and then I get sad. I wish I could get more pissed off because I don't get mad enough. I'm very numb about K. I don't even see him as a person. He's dead, he's been dead for some time, but it wouldn't matter. I have no feeling for him at all.

Because of the incest survivor treatment, I have an understanding of why I'm the way I am today. There's a lot I have to work on still. I'm new at recovery in this area. I know I'm supposed to get angry. I can't get angry at my family. I get angry when other people are describing their parents; I want to kill them with a gun or murder them, but I can't feel that way toward my parents, so I know that has to be worked on. I'm just letting it come.

Notes on your reaction to Courtney's Story:

What images, thoughts, or feelings were triggered in you by reading Courney's story? Even if you're not chemically dependent, were any of the feelings similar?

4 *Feeling the*

Feelings:

Grief and Rage

PHASES OF RECOVERY

After breaking denial, which allows some partial or full recall experiences, it's time to let the feelings come up. Many survivors at this point begin to grieve, feeling an overwhelming sadness. Others find themselves feeling angry for a while, in a perpetual rage. You need to know that these reactions are natural and expectable; their emergence signals the positive release of feelings that you were previously unable to process.

It's important to allow yourself to experience these emotions fully and completely. They will cleanse and free you. Some survivors try to move directly to forgiveness without experiencing these negative emotions, but this can delay the healing. You can't recover just by thinking about it or by intellectually understanding the recovery process. There are layers of feelings you have avoided, and they must be faced without denial, without drugs, alcohol, or other numbing behavior. This is why it is so important to be clean and sober, and why building your support system is essential; this is the value of knowing what help is available and how to get it.

As you learn to experience your emotions, you will need to learn how to comfort yourself, how to tell yourself that you possess the inner resources and self-esteem to make it through them. This is done by working with the vulnerable part of your psyche, the "little child" in you. Such Inner Child work is the subject of the next chapter.

Remember, each recovery process is unique. You may be ready at this point to read about grieving, or you may prefer to get in touch with your Inner Child. Your anger might emerge before you can acknowledge your vulnerability. Read this chapter and the next in whatever order you need to, knowing that you can come back to them again and again.

GRIEVING

Once your amnesia lifts or when you first identify that you were molested as a child, it is normal to feel tremendous sadness and to feel as if you're walking around in a daze. Things that used to be easy may become harder. Many survivors enter a period in which it is hard to go through the motions of life, to go to work, to go out into the world. Don't panic. This is a temporary stage and it will pass. You are integrating information that you blocked out in order to survive and keep going. You are now learning to function and carry this new information at the same time.

Many survivors are afraid that if they let themselves feel sad, they'll get lost in it. You need to know that you can move into the pain and move back out again. However, there is a critical distinction between depression and sadness, self-pity and grieving. This is particularly true for the recovering alcoholic incest survivor, because self-pity can cause you to start drinking again, but refusing to allow yourself to grieve can also trigger a relapse. Self-pity is typically characterized by a feeling of "I'm the only one who's ever gone through this; I'm all alone and I'll always be all alone," and a morose, repetitive focus on the self. If we're honest, there may even be a secret sense of pleasure in self-pity, a self-indulgence. This is hard to admit, and it takes time to learn to distinguish between self-pity and true sadness that is an appropriate response to loss. In comparison, grieving is simply an honest self-appraisal that says, "I'm sad right now," or "My heart hurts," or "I have an ache inside."

The feeling tone around this kind of pain is: "I have a right to be sad. The rest of the world has its pain and this is mine. I won't compare or exaggerate my pain, but I won't diminish it. I will stay with it until it is done."

To deny this feeling or to refuse to put it into words can only make you vulnerable to act out the pain, whether you do this with chemical dependency, self-mutilation, destructive relationships, or getting someone else to abuse you or abandon you. Just like children unable to put their feelings into words, we must act out what we can't say. So, although you may feel temporarily like you've "lost" your control, power comes from surrendering to what is true, owning it, and claiming it as part of your reality.

When the grief hits, the need for several supportive people in your life becomes more apparent. You are going through a period where you may feel you need people desperately. This is understandable, but if you spend a lot of time with one person you may worry that you will "burn them out." One answer to this is to find several people who can be supportive so that you can allow yourself to be as dependent as you need to be but spread it around. Three people can handle your needs much better than one, because they each have a smaller piece of it; ten people can handle it even better.

During your time of grieving, allow yourself to move more slowly. Take on as few commitments as possible. You have suffered a loss. It is similar to what people go through in response to the death of a loved one or in adjusting to an injury to the body. You have lost your innocence and a part of your childhood. This is a loss to your sense of self, and you have a right to grieve it.

Allow yourself time to be alone, to not have to be "on" for anybody. You also may find comfort in keeping some low-stress structure in your life, something to "show up" for that does not demand too much from you: a minimally occupying job, going to the movies, sitting in a café or a park, just to get out of the house.

Sometimes being in the proximity of people is useful if you don't feel up to making social plans with others. This helps to take your focus off yourself and your pain just long enough to give you a breather, so there's a balance inside.

Some survivors feel as if they are "falling apart" because they cry easily. Crying is therapeutic; it is an essential part of working through your grief. Someone once said that tears mean your heart is thawing from its hardened state. Just carry around some extra tissues. Pull off to the side of the road if you are driving. If you wish, call people who understand and can just listen and respond softly to your tears and crying sounds. They are not ugly sounds. You are not a "drag to be around" to people who have experienced their own grief in some way. You will probably find that people are a lot more compassionate than you give them credit for.

You may find that your definition of a friend is changing as you discover that someone you thought was reliable lets you down, and that someone else you never expected to be there shows up and says the perfect thing at the perfect time. You may be acquiring a whole new set of friends and letting go of some old ones. You may have a sense of searching, scanning the environment for somebody to feel safe with, and a craving for a relationship that has a sense of history to it, one in which you don't have to explain anything and can just "be." Sometimes there's a restlessness and irritability as if "nothing's right." Wherever you are, you wish you were somewhere else: When you're alone, you want to be with people, and when you're with people, you want to be alone.

Ask yourself what you need and try to provide whatever it is, unless it would hurt you or someone else. If you could have exactly what you wanted right now, what would it be? Going to sleep, getting under the covers, watching a movie, eating soup, and drinking tea are a few examples of nurturing activities. The task at this point is to build in a sense of comforting. Take time out of every day to be with yourself in a quiet way. Take walks, be near water, look at nature, art, or beautiful, timeless things—anything that gives you a sense of order and security. Listen to Bach or George Winston, curl up by a fireplace and watch the flames dance.

How to Survive the Loss of a Love by Melba Colgrove, Harold Bloomfield, and Peter McWilliams, a small book filled with comforting suggestions and poems on the grieving process, is an excellent book to read during this time.

PROCESSES FOR GRIEVING

Body Work

Discover where you're holding the sadness in your body. Does it settle in any particular place or is it generalized and pervasive? What's happening in your throat, chest, stomach, and particularly around your heart? Is there a pressure, an ache, a piercing pain, or a feeling of being doubled over with pain? If you could sit with that feeling for a few minutes and allow your body to do what it wants, what would it do? Lie down, curl up into a ball, pace, rock, cry, scream, wail?

In Jerry Mason's book called *The Family of Women*, on page 182, there are some beautiful pictures of women grieving. If you look at these women from all over the world, their facial expressions and body postures take on a similarity that gives a universal sense to the emotion of grieving. Other more "primitive" cultures are much more sane and sophisticated than ours in their allowance for and understanding of the need for rituals and time for people to grieve.

Lean into the pain. Embrace it. Let it be. There is something else underneath that will rise up if you will let yourself pass though this layer. You may discover other feelings along the way, but somewhere at the core of you, something is working to heal itself.

Reaching Out

Pick up the phone and call someone and tell them how you're feeling. Don't expect people to guess what is going on inside you. Ask for help. Make a request for time or whatever you feel you need. It might sound something like: "I'm feeling lost, scared, sad, (etc.). I need someone to just listen to me for a minute. Is that okay with you?" If you get answering machines, leave messages, asking people to call you back. Keep calling until you reach someone. If all else fails, most communities have a grief hot line where someone is available twenty-four hours a day. Don't hesitate to go to any lengths on your own behalf. You have suffered alone long enough.

Learning to Comfort Yourself

Be your own source of comfort. Lie down and breathe into the spot in your body where you hold the pain. Experiment with different rates and depths of breathing, and see if you can help yourself open your throat and upper chest. Picture a gold or pink band of light pouring down into you, bathing you and filling your body with a warm glow. Visualize comforting scenes.

Anything approximating a feeling of being held may be very useful right now. You can wrap yourself up in a blanket, use the warm water of a bath, lie in a hammock, or rock yourself gently in a rocking chair. Find a spot outside somewhere that feels safe, get an old blanket and lie on the ground, feeling the solidity of the earth underneath you. Let yourself sink into it and let it hold you as you draw strength from it. Put your hand over your heart and feel the warmth from your palm sinking into your chest or whatever place inside you is hurting. Repeat loving, reassuring messages to yourself, over and over: "It's going to be okay. I'm right here. I'm not leaving you. I will never leave you and I will never let anyone hurt you, ever again. It's okay; everything's going to be all right. You don't have to be afraid or alone anymore." (See the "Affirmations" section below and the "Mother Love Affirmations" section of Chapter Five on "Working with the Inner Child.")

Establish New Rituals

There may be times in the day when it is particularly difficult to function—mornings and nights may be especially hard. This is a time when your psyche is most vulnerable, when you don't have your defenses as firmly in place.

Mornings and evenings can be a good time to read something positive or to work on your affirmations. Get a pretty journal and set up a place in your house and a time in your morning when you can read or write for fifteen or thirty minutes before you go on about your day. Create some comforting rituals, things that the "little girl" in you likes: hot chocolate at bedtime, or settling into bed with a spiritual book or a good "escape" book.

Affirmations—Changing the Belief Systems Daily

Experiencing depression is a part of the grieving process, but it can also be the end result of holding in anger. When you are depressed you may have recurring negative thoughts, such as, "My life is a mess. It's always been a mess and it's always going to be this way." Affirmations—reassuring phrases that you repeat to yourself—can give you a lift; they can't eliminate the necessary process of feeling the feelings and integrating them into your personality, but they can redirect your energy if you are spiraling downward.

To use an affirmation, you simply insert your name in the affirmation and say it (or tape it and listen to it while you're driving, for example). Say it over and over until you feel a shift inside. Here are some examples of affirmations:

"I, _____(your name)_____, am getting better and better. I will make it through this."

"There is a purpose and a plan for my life. I,

_____ , am on the road to recovery."

"I, _____, made it through the experience of incest. I can make it through the memories."

"I, _____, am now surrounded by loving guides to help me."

"It is now safe for me, _____, to be in this world and in this body."

"I, _____, am a lovable, beautiful woman."

"I, _____, trust myself to take care of myself."

I Deserve Love, by Sondra Ray, offers more examples of affirmations about self-love.

Affirmations with a Negative Response Column

Divide a piece of paper in half, lengthwise. Write the affirmation on the left side and then listen to what your mind says about it. Whatever it is, write down your negative response and then write the affirmation again. Write your response. Keep repeating this process until your mind agrees with the affirmation, even if begrudgingly.

Affirmation	**Response**
"I, ____(your name)____, am a lovable human being."	"This will never work."
"I, _____, am a lovable human being."	"This is ridiculous, how can it help?"
"I, _____, am a lovable human being."	"You're never going to get any better. You're sick and you're worthless."
"I, _____, am a lovable human being."	"Well, maybe you're not that bad."
"I, _____, am a lovable human being."	"Well, you did do something nice for yourself the other day."
"I, _____, am a lovable human being."	"Maybe."

Keep writing until you get some resonance between the columns.

Self-Care Commitment

If you are going to survive the grieving stage, you must make a commitment to your own self-care. Others can

116

help, but you have to choose to do something to take good care of yourself every day. The concept of comforting yourself is foreign to most survivors, and you may have to train yourself to listen to what you need and give it to yourself without withholding or self-criticizing. Ask yourself now:

What feels comforting to me? (Be specific.)

_____

I commit to taking care of myself during my grieving process in the following ways:

_____

I will do them at these times:

_____

One-Week Check-In

How did I do with my commitment?

_____

What did I let interfere?

_____

If you weren't able to keep your self-care commitment, simply make a new commitment and try again.

117

My new commitment is: _____

_____

The person I'm going to tell about my self-care commitment and get back to with a progress report is:

_____

INCREASING YOUR SUPPORT SYSTEM

Building a support system is absolutely essential to incest recovery. As you begin to establish this system and the other personal relationships in your life, know that it's okay not to have deep, intimate contact right away or with everyone you know.

Survivors of childhood abuse tend to have difficulty with boundaries—understandably, since this is precisely what the incest violated. They may have a tendency to alternate between being isolated and withdrawn, on the one hand, and, on the other, having no boundaries, thereby bombarding others with their feelings and needs before a relationship has had a chance to build to a level of trust that can hold the intimacy. Sometimes survivors hold everything in from everybody, and then feel so lonely that they blurt everything out to someone they barely know. The result is that they may then feel embarrassed to speak to the new friend again, feeling overexposed and fearing they've overwhelmed the other person.

Remember that bonding takes time and needs a balance of opening and closing: opening, to share and receive information about each other, and closing, for time to assimilate it. If you are creating a new relationship with someone, you have to build a history with them. It's only by repeatedly spending time together that you can increase your familiarity with each other and feel more and more comfortable being together. There is no substitute for friends you've known for years and there are no shortcuts.

Building a support system starts with exposure: How often do you get out of the house? Where do you go? What do you do? It sometimes helps to choose some structured settings such as incest survivor groups or workshops, or Twelve Step meetings to meet new people, so you already share a common base and purpose on which to found a new relationship.

The next steps are making eye contact, moving into closer physical proximity, and saying "Hi." These steps are especially important to survivors, since many have taught themselves to "go invisible" at will. They can be standing in front of people and remain virtually unnoticed. How are you dressed? Do you have your head down? Do you avoid eye contact? What are you signaling to people nonverbally? If you want people to leave you alone, they probably will. If you want human contact, you have to open yourself to it. You can quit whenever you want, but if you're used to isolating yourself, it's a good idea to stretch your tolerance for being noticed and paid attention to, particularly in a healthy, safe environment. You can always shut down again, but see if you can let somebody in a little bit before you do.

The Little Prince is a treasure of a book that you might want to get from the library and read at this point. It describes a process called "taming": The Little Prince and the gray fox sit side by side every day, in the same place at the same time, and gradually, wordlessly, a bond grows between them. There's a great deal of wisdom in this tale because, to a large degree, you don't really have to do anything more than this to form a relationship with another human being. By repeatedly spending time together, over a period, you can't help bonding with someone, at least on a social level, unless you actively choose to prevent it.

The next phase is moving to a level of increased intimacy, from "social bonding" to a more personal or individual bond. Some survivors find this very awkward and even scary. Just remember, you are only testing the water to see if the other person is open to increasing the contact. All you have to do is throw a line out. If there's no response, you can move on. On the other hand, don't be surprised to find that the other person is more awkward and shy than you are and is relieved that you took the initiative.

You can use anything from social chatter such as, "I like your hat. I used to have one like it," to "I've been noticing you come here often. I wonder if I could talk to you more. Could we talk on the phone sometime?"

If the latter feels too risky, simply continue to chat, letting the other person know you're noticing something special about him or her and identifying with it in some way. This is a perfectly acceptable and appropriate form of getting to know someone. After a few trials at this, you may be ready to talk about something more personal, such as a feeling or experience that's a little more current or "real."

The next phase is making a plan for spending time together one to one, even if it's on the phone. This may involve getting and giving phone numbers, and then calling to ask "How are you?"

There are two important parts in this simple exchange. First, asking questions about the other, then sharing something about yourself.

There is a process in ACA recovery called "share-test-share." This is done by revealing a little bit about yourself to see how the other person responds. If you get a positive response, share more. If you don't like the new person's response to your self-disclosure, shift back into the "social friend" expectation, and move on to someone else to open up on a deeper level.

The purpose of the next phase is to find out more about the other person. Things you might choose to do include calling again, having a cup of coffee together, or asking for time, perhaps an hour or an hour and a half at first, to have lunch together or to do some fun things, such as going for a walk or to a movie.

Those not practiced in developing relationships may go from isolation to compulsive caretaking, choosing only friends who have more problems than they do, so that they can always be the one relied on for advice and support. This can be an act of service and love, or it can be a form of control and a way to avoid healthy risks or to avoid allowing oneself to be on the receiving end. If you are always on the giving end of a relationship, it's unusual if it does not eventually build resentment on your part and a feeling of being depleted.

The goal at this time in your recovery is to have at least some mutually supportive, mutually beneficial relationships. If you've been isolated for a while, you may need to operate on the "somebody, anybody" philosophy at first, and progressively become more selective about the people you choose as friends. Increasing your skill at assessing others' levels of functioning before entering into relationships with them can save a lot of time and energy. You can be reassured that this is a skill you will acquire over time.

Healthy people have conditions and criteria for what they want in a friendship. Their criteria usually include the other's professional abilities or interests, spiritual beliefs, social skills, and intellectual compatibility. Ask yourself, "How much fun do we have when we're together?" For example, do you laugh together?

Observe how you match with the other person in these and other areas, and learn your own priorities. Which of these areas can you compromise on and which not? Your time and energy are limited and precious. You don't have to like everybody, and it's okay to say no to someone who wants to be your friend if you don't feel that you're getting enough back. Many relationship conflicts can be traced back to errors in the selection procedure and can be avoided by really knowing yourself—what you want and what you have to offer—and not underselling yourself.

Once you've established a rapport with a person, you need to nourish that relationship. Friendship maintenance is not taking people for granted, but expressing appreciation for the things you like about them—who they are and what they do.

Relationship upkeep is doing things like:

Check-ins, reporting back on how an event turned out that you got some help on from your friend

Follow-through on things you've offered, or at least cancel if you are unable to do it

Planning ahead, inviting your friend to events

Thinking up things that the other would enjoy, or that would be fun to do together

Gifts, cards

Remembering special events in each other's lives and celebrating together

Reminiscing and creating new memories

PROCESSES FOR INCREASING YOUR SUPPORT SYSTEM

Whom can I call? _____

When? _____

When I'm feeling a little more "together," the person I'm going to try to reach out to, to see if they're willing to be there for me when the grief hits again: _____

Who feels safe? _____

Whom do I admire and want to invite into my life so that I can learn something from them? _____

What kind of activities do I want to be doing with somebody? _____

What is fun for me? Who do I know who might be interested in something like that? _____

Who seems as if they'd be a good friend to do fun things with? _____

EXPRESSING AND RELEASING RAGE

The day will come when you begin to contact your anger. For some people, this is the first stage; for others, it comes after the grieving. Whenever it comes, you may wake up feeling enraged, day after day. Incidents that nobody else seems to notice may leave you wanting to scream. You may feel like yelling at people, driving your car in a crazy way, or wanting to hurt or kill someone.

You are not crazy for feeling like this. You don't have to hurt yourself or anyone with these feelings. Rage is a natural and healthy response to being violated, and it will allow you to get more in touch with your power. As a child, you probably were not allowed to express this rage, so when you first begin to let it come up, you may be dealing with years of "stuffed" anger. If you keep expressing and releasing the feelings, they will become less intense. Just keep moving them out of your body. One of the primary benefits of discharging all the old anger is being able to respond to current issues with less "emotional charge," because you haven't accumulated a load of pent-up emotion.

Many people have held in crying and yelling for so long that even when the feelings surface they feel unable to let them out. Some people have received messages from their families that it is shameful to show feelings publicly. For these people it becomes especially difficult to share feelings in the presence of others.

When we are threatened, the central nervous system produces adrenaline to prepare us for "fight or flight." Incest survivors and other Post-traumatic Stress Disorder survivors have learned to live with very high levels of fear and anger in their bodies, from years of hypervigilance and anticipating unpredictable, dangerous events.

Once our bodies have produced this adrenaline, it is difficult to release it through talking alone. It is necessary to express the feelings through physical movement or a deep, specific kind of breathing. Therapists who specialize in body work—such as bioenergetics, Reichean work, integrative body programming, or rebirthing—teach clients to release feelings by working with the body and/or the breath.

The theory and technique these therapists use vary

somewhat, but the basic idea is to identify where you have held feelings in your body in chronic and habitual patterns. This is said to cause bands of muscular tightening, called "armoring," that make it difficult to allow those feelings out, even if you want to. For example, if you're feeling sad and you want to cry but nothing comes out, there is a particular place that you hold the sadness, such as your jaw, throat or chest. The therapist helps you locate where you are "armored" and then, through teaching you to breathe, positioning your body, and, in some cases, using pressure points or deep tissue massage, helps you to release stored feelings out of the body. Sometimes repressed memories come up spontaneously during this work as well.

There is some evidence that armoring contributes to physical illnesses, especially in long-term cases. (See *Love Is Letting Go of Fear*, by Gerald Jampolski, and the research by the Center for Attitudinal Healing on healing cancer and other life-threatening illnesses by releasing anger and working with forgiveness.)

If you have any physical illness symptoms that haven't yielded to traditional medical help or if you've been involved in "talking therapies" for a while and are feeling stuck, you may want to consider some of these alternative therapies that take the whole body into account. It is my belief that if you decide to do this deep release work, it's important to establish contact with the therapist in addition to achieving the emotional release itself. For example, if you've been working with your eyes closed or in a partial trance state, you need to come out of it to make eye contact with your therapist at some point in your expressing and releasing to let that person be there with you, while you are feeling or when you are reliving the traumatic event. Recovery comes through reexperiencing the trauma or repressed feeling with an ally. (See *Body, Self and Soul: Sustaining Integration*, by Jack Rosenberg, for more information.)

Use your inner guidance on whether this type of therapy is right for you and whom you trust to do it, particularly when there is the possibility of any kind of touch between you and your body worker. Physical contact may feel too intrusive at one stage of your recovery, while it may feel freeing and comforting at another time.

Use the processes in this section to keep clearing the anger from your body. Keep clearing and clearing; express and release. Move the energy. Remember, you have a choice to break through or break down. *Breakthrough* is the experience of releasing feelings and opening up to a new level of understanding and acceptance; *breakdown* is feeling immobilized and victimized.

PROCESSES FOR RELEASING RAGE: BODY WORK

If possible, these exercises are best done in the presence of another person or your therapist. If you're not ready for that, begin on your own and, as you get more comfortable with feeling and expressing your anger, consider asking another person to work with you.

The following are some tools for expressing anger—letting it out and getting rid of it so that you can move on to the next phase.

Beat Pillows

Find a room that is relatively private and pile up a bunch of pillows on the floor. If possible, put a futon or mattress underneath the pillows. Sit on your knees in front of them and begin to take some slow deep breaths. Then begin to take shorter breaths, allowing a sound to come out if you want. Raise both arms over your head, hands clenched into fists, and drop them down into the pillows. Make sure there are enough pillows that you don't hurt your hands. Repeat this procedure with intensifying energy, letting out sounds if you want. If you can, get someone to sit in front of you to hold the pillows and keep them from moving around.

Keep letting go into the pillows, allowing yourself to move your feelings out of your body. Allow memories, pictures, and images of the person you are mad at to come into your mind while you are letting the energy move out of your arms and hands.

Variations: Lie down on your bed or on a futon on the floor and do the same breathing as before. Still lying down, raise your arms up over your head and bring them down by your sides, hard, into the mattress or futon. Pile pillows under your feet and kick your feet into them.

Power Stomp/Power Walk

When taking a walk, picture the person you hate. Now picture stomping on them with your feet. Push the angry energy onto the pavement or dirt and down into the earth. Use as much visual imagery as you like. Here are a few images that other survivors have come up with when doing this process:

Wearing cleats on your feet and stepping on the person you hate

Smashing the perpetrator's body

Screaming at the offender and humiliating him

Pushing the offender down a flight of stairs and being able to stand at the top and look down

This may feel scary at first, but in reality you are not hurting anybody by doing this. In fact, you may be preventing yourself from hurting yourself or someone you love by taking responsibility for redirecting your anger.

Hand Scream

Take a few deep breaths. Then, covering your mouth with a hand or pillow, scream into it, either with sound or just air. Keep pushing the air out in one long breath until you feel out of breath or a little dizzy. Breathe in and then try again, trying to go a little further every time. Finish with more deep breaths.

This is a good exercise to use when you're at work or in a public place where you can't make a lot of noise. If something makes you mad during the day, instead of stuffing it you can always excuse yourself to the rest room, and do a few hand screams. This will allow you to feel energized instead of depleted.

PROCESS: WRITING OUT THE RAGE

In addition to keeping a journal of your dreams and/or feelings, do your feelings ever want to take the form of stories or poems? Are you haunted by an image that you could put down in words, simply describing what you see? Sometimes this descriptive writing takes on a powerful, raw, poetic quality that is very moving to read.

Triumph over Darkness, by Wendy Wood and Leslie Hatton, is a beautiful collection of women survivors' art and poetry. The following is an example of a powerful piece of poetry from that book.

For Father's Day

To my dad.
Never been a child
just born
never been a child
just fucked.
Didn't talk too much
just watched a lot
learned a lot.
Wild but tamed

never been little.
But I knew how to play the game.
Mom always told me
your dad has needs
I can't meet them all
but you can, so be a good little girl,
He's been through a lot.
Anyway, you got it good.
My pale face mother
stupid white bitch.
She gets what she wants by letting others shit
    on her.
It makes her feel like she's worth something,
and she's been a good wife.
Daddy sure loved her, according to her.
But mom, what about all those other women in
    his life?
Oh, they're just friends of his, helpless women.
He feels sorry for them and takes care of
    them.
Most of them are widows.
Not to speak of me, my sisters, their friends,
    and mine.
Great love, a father who takes care of every
    woman's needs.
Oh mighty fuck, father fuck, oh best fuck of the
    world, super stud.
Save the Indian race, fuck the chief
never satisfied
had to fuck till it finally fell off.
Cancer you say?
Are you satisfied?

Did you finally come daddy?
I'm tired, leave me alone.

> *With hate, in rage and anger,*
> *your daughter,*
> ***KYOS***

Here are two other poems by another survivor, Kathy Duby, that illustrate the feelings of frozen grief and the pain of not being allowed to have your childhood.

You be the mommy and I'll be the baby
You slap me, and yell at me, and hurt me
I won't cry.
You starve me, and punch me, and kick me
I won't cry.
You hurt me, and hate me, and hit me
I won't cry.
I'll be a good baby.

You be the baby and I'll be the mommy
I'll burn you and drop you and throw you
And see how you like it.
I'll ignore you and forget to change your diaper
*   and forget to feed you*
And see how you like it.
I'll leave you outside in your carriage in the rain
*   while I pass out*
And see how you like it.
I'll be a bad mommy.

You be the mommy and I'll be the baby

You love me and take care of me and smile at me
*   and feel happy you have me*
I need a good mommy.

Kathy Duby

Riding in the limousine
Following the hearse
That carries my dead sister
To the cemetery
Holding my breath
Worried about bumps, potholes
That would jostle her, hurt her
Not letting her be dead
Worried she could be hurt
Not feeling my own hurt

Riding in the limousine
Following my sister
On the way to bury her
A policeman stands
Hat over his heart
Waving us through the intersection
Honoring my dead sister
Who he never met
I am lost now
No one will ever see me
As she did

Riding in the limousine
A long line of cars behind us
Their lights on, though it is noon

Lighting the way
To the cemetery
My dead sister
Is really dead

Riding in the limousine
I couldn't cry
Holding my breath
My siblings beside me
All separate, alone
Holding in our grief
Holding in our tears
Holding in our pain
A lesson we learned well

Don't cry
Don't ever cry
Don't be a baby
Don't you dare cry
Even when
Riding in a limousine
Following the hearse
That carries my dead sister

Kathy Duby

PROCESS: DRAWING OUT THE RAGE

Get yourself a big piece of blank paper and some crayons.

Choose a color and a shape to show what it feels like in your body right now. Use a free-form approach. Anything is okay—this is purely for you. There are no right or wrong ways; you can't make a mistake.

Color what your hurt looks like.

Color what your rage looks like.

Draw a picture of yourself.

Draw your Inner child (see Chapter Five)

Draw your family.

If you're in therapy, it's a great idea to make some drawings at the beginning, on each of these five issues, and then draw them again at three months, six months, and a year of recovery. Look back at the series and see if you notice any changes.

Another idea is to draw out a floor plan of your family's house. Where is your room; where did you spend the most time? Where is your parents' room and where did each of them sleep? Where are your siblings' rooms? Who slept with whom, and at what ages? What does it feel like to walk back into your old house through this technique?

The drawings on pages 138, 139, and 141 show how some survivors perceive themselves. The first two were done by survivors in early stages of recovery; the third has been in recovery longer.

The first drawing (see page 138) reflects this woman's feelings of extreme vulnerability and shame (face turned away) and a sense of "hanging" in an unstable world. The person she drew is clearly a child and portrays her sense of herself as young, unprepared for life, supported precariously but with no feet on the ground and no ground to fall onto. There is a lot of detail and the fingers look as if they're holding on tight to the ropes of the swing, which are the most defined item in the picture. The person's boundaries are fairly weak, as seen in the light, tentative sketch style, but the figure is clothed and has on shoes. There is an air of wistfulness, tentativeness, and inhibition about the picture, like someone who could never quite allow herself to be seen as a child. Figures drawn with no clothes or shoes indicate a weaker sense of boundaries. There is less separation between the person who is unclothed and the world. It also indicates a more primitive formulation of body image, more typical of the drawing of a younger child.

The second drawing (see page 139) shows extreme distress and a sense of paralysis and victimization, as shown in the sentences the woman wrote alongside the person, saying, "I can't move, Failure, I've got to, I can't, I can, I can't." There is a representation of what looks like a ray of hope going from the person to the sun up in the right-hand corner. The face and the posts of the bed are heavily detailed, as compared to the lack of detail or even delineation of any other body parts, such as arms, legs, hands, fingers, or any kind of impression about a sexually developed body. All body parts and features are covered in blankets. There is a slight impression of arms and a lump under the covers, which may be the feet, but they are not an active part of the picture, indicating this woman's lack of a feeling connection with her own body, and possibly a strong tendency to disassociate. The general impression given by the drawing is that this person wants and needs to hide from life. The figure lying in bed under blankets indicates that early dependency needs have not been met, and that the woman requires more "holding" and safety to proceed developmentally to a time where she can feel powerful and self-sufficient.

The third drawing (see page 141) suggests a strong sense of self in the heavy outline of the body image. There is a lot of detail in the figure's shoes (with laces), fingers, clothes (especially the collar and belt), and facial features (particularly the eyebrows). The figure is standing in a clearly defined doorway and at what looks like the beginning of a path. There is a sense of great determination and hopefulness, as if she is experiencing strength in her strong shoulders and thick legs. The little feet and small, less well-defined hands may indicate a hidden sense of fragility and a feeling of ineffectiveness in the world.

CONFRONTING THE FAMILY

After working through your rage, there may come a time when it feels appropriate to confront your family. This is a very big step and should be carefully planned and thought through before you take any action. It is a very good idea to get a lot of support while making up your game plan, including input and feedback from others who are familiar with your situation, particularly your therapist. Know what you want for yourself. Here are some questions to consider:

What do you want to get out of this step?

What are the potential consequences of confronting the family?

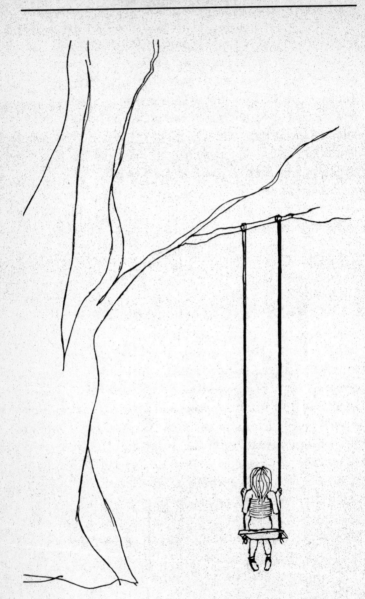

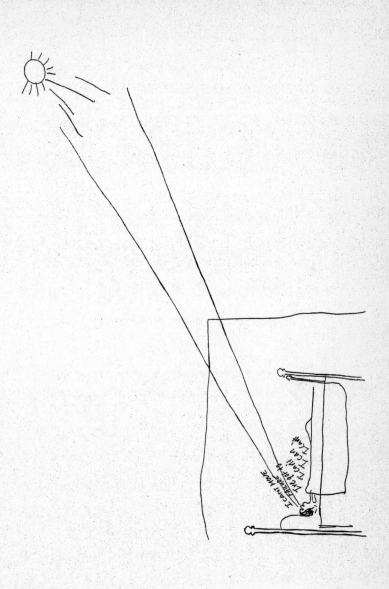

Are you ready and willing to face them?

What are the possible losses?

What childhood hopes and fantasies do you need to relinquish in order to do this? For example, is there any residual hope that someday, somehow, somebody in your family is going to make up for the abuse you've suffered?

Are you ready to release the hope forever?

Do you face losing some kind of nurturing contact with some family member(s) whom you love by breaking the code of silence?

Are you ready to let it go?

Do you have replacements?

Are there possible financial losses?

Who needs to be confronted?

Who do you want to start with? Who is the safest person to approach? Who are you most afraid to confront?

What kind of support do you need for yourself when making these decisions?

What kind of support do you need before and after the confrontation?

Do you need the help of a therapist?

Do you need a friend to go with you or be with you directly afterward?

What's the worst thing that could happen?

What's the best thing?

Are you being realistic?

What is your worst fear?

Is the person you are confronting violent?

Are you putting yourself at risk by talking to him or her?

What would it be like if you did not confront that person?

Is the family sober? Is it possible to have any kind of useful communication as long as the family members are in active addictions?

Important:

Are there any children currently at risk of being abused?

What are the child abuse reporting laws in your state?

Do you want to make a legal report? Do you need more information/support to make that decision?

Your therapist and/or your community mental health agency should be knowledgeable and supportive about helping you define these things and sort out your choices. Also, most cities have a local child protective services office that can let you know about these issues, if you'd prefer to ask some questions anonymously.

Parents United groups include a phase in which survivors can be in a group with perpetrators. This can be a useful process for many women who wish to practice confrontation in a safe way.

After considering the questions above, you will be more prepared to make a good decision, for yourself and your family. Pay particular attention to the question "What is the worst thing that could happen?" Get some help on evaluating whether your answer to this is your Inner Child's fear or a realistic appraisal of potential danger or loss.

Some survivors have been tremendously empowered by confronting first their fear and then the perpetrator and/or the "nonoffending" parent, the legal term for the spouse. I prefer the term "collusive" parent and/or siblings, because on some level there is an agreement between the other family members not to expose the incest. This is why the incest goes on despite the fact that the survivor has usually left a trail of signals asking for help.

Even if the perpetrator and others completely deny the incest, sometimes just knowing that she has broken the silence and stood up for her Inner Child is tremendously healing for a survivor. For others, it never feels safe to make an actual confrontation, but it is still possible to recreate the scenario through psychodrama or by using the "empty chair" technique: In the presence of an understanding friend or therapist, you visualize the person you want to confront sitting in an empty chair next to yours. Say what you want to say to them, imagining how they would react. Then switch chairs and take on the confronted person's personality and body posture and respond to your confrontation as you think they would. Keep moving back and forth in the chair until you feel the dialogue is complete.

Read the following survivor's experiences of her attempt to confront her family, and how getting an appropriate response from her mother evolved over a long period of time.

ISADORA'S STORY

Introduction

Isadora's recovery has occurred in layers, moving from the breaking-denial stage to anger work with groups and her own self-education. She has used her painful life experiences as fuel for her determination to succeed, both personally and professionally. She has pushed herself to excellence and used her pain as a source of inspiration and willingness to help others. Even when she became the victim of a random mugging in the midst of her recovery, she didn't cave in. Rather, she continued working on her healing and moved to a deeper level of release through breathing and body-work therapy.

Isadora is a single thirty-eight-year-old woman, of

Caucasian and Hispanic backgrounds, with her own professional practice as a doctor. She is extremely bright, verbal, confident, and attractive. She has one brother, nine years older. Her parents, both alcoholics, divorced before she was five.

Isadora was molested by her older brother from ages four to eleven; the molestation included fondling and oral sex. Her brother also physically abused her. His abuse of Isadora ended when he was told to move out of the house by their new stepfather, who then began to molest Isadora himself from the time she was thirteen until she was sixteen years of age.

As a teenager, Isadora abused drugs and alcohol, ran away, and prostituted herself, but never became suicidal or self-mutilated in any way.

Memories of the incest with her brother began to surface for Isadora after major surgery at age twenty-four, and she began going to women's consciousness-raising groups that included incest survivors. She then went on to pursue professional training as a psychiatrist and, coincidentally, her clients began to bring in incest material. She feels that working with her clients has enabled her to resolve many of her own residual issues.

Isadora is currently in touch with her family. Both her mother and stepfather are sober in AA now for more than twenty years. She and her mother are writing a book together about their mutual experience of the sexual abuse. Isadora sees the molestation as a chain of abuse that victimized her parents as well as herself.

In her recovery, Isadora has drawn on a wide variety of resources. Over a period of ten years, she has read extensively, gone to many types of therapy groups, been involved in a Twelve Step program (ACA) and self-help groups, and has incorporated her knowledge of incest into her work with others. She is currently going to a therapist who works on body armoring, using breath work and the support of the relationship to release feelings. She is a powerful and beautiful woman, who articulates and embodies the spirit of a fully recovering person.

Isadora's Story

It's hard to remember the sequence of the abusive events in my life. However, the older and more "cured" I get, the more I remember, and some of the larger gaps are now filled. Some of my first memories are: deep knife cuts on the front door of our apartment; my teenage brother and his friends, loud and raucous, breaking the few toys I had; a pillow pushed over my face until I remembered no more. Kneeling between his legs as he lay on my mother's bed. I remember my neck aching and sore from moving to the monotonous rhythm of his sex. I remember throwing up his come in the bathroom sink and believing that he had been nice to me by not making me swallow it. I can see large bruises on my body, particularly on my upper arms where he would hit me repeatedly, wait for the bruises to form, and then hit me in the same spot again after the appropriate coloration produced the desired target.

I remember him holding my cat by its paws, hanging it out the third-story window, laughing. I remember him offering me to his friends, and making me and my best friend fight, hard, in front of him. I can see him standing naked before me, licking me, asking me if I liked it, and I did. He would come home late at night and enter our room smelling of alcohol. I remember the smell of his vomit on the rug below the bunk bed where I slept. I would leave home early in the morning before he woke up, feeling free for a little while to play alone in the fog at the park. I'd call home in the evening to be sure Mom was there before I came back. Once my brother told me Mom was home and then he met me at the door with a belt.

My mother had lots of beautiful and exotic shoes in her closet. One time I fried up a lot of insects and left them in a pair of her beautiful slippers. I broke a boy's nose with my skate; I bit the end of my friend's finger off in a fist fight. I lied and I stole. I was hungry and cold a lot. I remember these things specifically between the ages of four or five and eight.

When I was ten or eleven, my mother married someone. He fed us and kicked my brother, who was then eighteen or nineteen, out of the house. I never liked my mother's husband, but I had my own room now and my brother was gone. This new man wanted to adopt me but I wouldn't let him. He did, however, change my name so that life would be easier for me. He only hit me sometimes. I had big boils on my butt. He'd lance them and show Mom what an act of love he was performing. When she left, he'd spread the lips of my vagina open and stare, and feel for boils.

He cried and said Mom didn't have sex with him anymore. When I was fourteen, he started coming into my room late at night, and I would awaken with my hand on his erect penis. I pretended to be asleep and I remember fear.

One night he woke me up and demanded to know who I had been having sex with. I was fifteen and it was my first love. If I didn't tell how we did it and what kind of birth control we used, he said he'd call my boyfriend's parents and tell them. Honesty, he said, was always the best. He took me to a gynecologist to make sure I wasn't pregnant. Then my stepfather moved us away from my boyfriend. We had venetian blinds in the new place, and the ones in my bedroom and bathroom were always a little askew. Sometimes I would hear him crunching in the leaves outside my bedroom window. When I came home from dates he would be waiting directly inside our front door, which had a peephole. I'd open the door and he'd be standing there, waiting and agitated, as I walked by.

At fifteen, maybe sixteen, I told my mom about him. She said she loved me, but that he was her husband and that I would be leaving home soon anyway. The priest was called in to talk to my stepfather. No one talked to me. Nothing changed except that I began an affair with my high school history teacher.

I left home at sixteen. I worked and went to school and went to school and worked. Sometimes I gave money to Mom. It seemed like money was always a problem. At seventeen I got pregnant. My boyfriend told my parents while I was in Mexico having an abortion, because he said he couldn't handle the pressure.

Mom said she would have raised my child herself, which, of course, set my guilt in.

There are times when I'm quite numb to the past and then there are other times when it hits me in that soft and vulnerable place and there's a great deal of sadness. Sometimes, it also produces a great deal of anger. At this point in my recovery, though, after I feel the feelings and let them pass through me, I almost always move to a deeper level of understanding.

I'm lucky, I think, that I've done a fair amount of therapy. The bulk of it started when I was around twenty-three. Then I started going to groups, women's groups, consciousness-raising groups, incest groups. Actually, at that time they weren't referred to as incest groups, but there were a lot of incest victims in the groups. I went to therapy off and on for about seven years. I went through periods of a great deal of anger. Then the next level of working through the abuse occurred in my late twenties and early thirties when I started getting professional cases. This was nothing that I'd planned for or anticipated; they just came to me. I found myself working through a lot of my own issues by dealing with my clients' issues. I studied the literature, reading everything on the subject of incest that I could get my hands on. And I consulted with therapists and people who were involved in the treatment field. That is still going on to this day.

Things were progressing very nicely in my life. I had my career and finally had some financial security. I also had a pretty solid understanding of my abuse and its effects on myself and other survivors. I had a good feeling about my life, that I was taking care of myself and contributing to the lives of others. Then I was kidnapped when I was thirty-five and that really brought up a lot of old feelings. The man wanted to kill me; he was a child molester. That got me back into individual therapy and got me into ACA and Al-Anon, where I learned about the concept of alcoholism as a disease and began the process of forgiving my family.

It's been through using ACA, individual therapy, educating myself, and working with other victims professionally that I've done a lot of healing. Recently, I started some body work, using a combination of physical therapy and mental and emotional work, and I feel as if I'm on the last layer of releasing the negative effects of these experiences and getting on about the business of having a full and wonderful life.

Notes on your reactions to Isadora's Story:

Was there anything in Isadora's story that you resonate with? What are your memories of sibling abuse? Was there any voyeurism or covert incest in your history?

5 | Working with
the Inner Child

As your feelings come to the surface, you will need to learn how to comfort yourself so that you are not overwhelmed. Comforting yourself means recognizing the emotional part of yourself and treating it with compassion and acceptance. It means reassuring the vulnerable part of yourself that you are willing and capable of your own support and protection.

Many people have found it helpful to picture their emotional self as a young child, so they can make these concepts more concrete and apply them on a daily basis. By visualizing your emotions as a child, you can more easily build a relationship with this aspect of yourself, learning to love and care for "her" until she comes to trust you. This may feel fragmenting at first, but it's a very good tool to allow you to recognize that part of yourself you need to recover—the Inner Child.

As you will discover from your Inner Child work, children are highly creative and resourceful beings if they have their security needs met. It is our Inner Child who is capable of the peak experiences. We need to be able to "regress in the service of the ego," as Freud said, in order to be completely "present" to a situation, to make love, to dream, to join, to feel ecstasy. We are all capable of this when the void inside is filled, and when the Child in us trusts us to take care of her physical needs. This will allow the Child to move through her own developmental milestones, now that she doesn't have to be obsessed with survival needs.

Until now, you may not have done a very good job of taking care of yourself or choosing healthy relationships. The Child is often angry at you or hiding, recoiled in a corner waiting to see what you're going to do next. Developing this relationship with your Inner Child is similar to the process an adoptive parent goes through, when he or she takes on the commitment to care for a child that has already experienced neglect, abuse, or the experience of being unwanted. The adoptive parent has to earn the child's trust and allow the child to test him or her. Providing love and consistency is the only way to build the trust.

Your Inner Child needs emotional connection and limits, or containment. Mother-love is the unconditional response to the child, the message that "You are okay, no matter what." Father-love says, "You can do it. I'm behind you. You can leave home and be successful in the world. Get out there and win."

One way to recognize the Inner Child is to think of times when you have been unreasonable—for example, when you were sulking, pouting, demanding, bashful, or showing off. Have you ever done things that made you wonder, "Where did that come from?" or that felt as if a secret part of you had sneaked out and surprised people who are otherwise accustomed to seeing your "adult"? This may manifest itself as not coming to work on time, losing track of time, and so forth. Observe these times and ask yourself if they occur more frequently when you've been neglecting your Child.

The Child often creates a crisis if she is ignored. Think about a real child who knows that she will have her needs met and that someone is there—then think of a whiny child. A child who expects to have her needs met can play contentedly, "check in" with a parent occasionally, and then go back to playing. A whiny child, on the other hand, has probably made repeated attempts to make contact with a parent and has been rejected or unheard. The natural response is to feel frustrated and demanding. Children have a basic human need called bonding. You might think of them as small airplanes that run out of fuel and have to land frequently, until they can accommodate a bigger tank. The child must make repeated contact with a parenting figure to know that there's somebody there, so that she can internalize this experience and develop a core sense of self, independent of contact with an external figure.

This entire process takes about eighteen to twenty years but is pivotally important in the first three to five years of life. If your primary caretakers were unavailable, alcoholic, or abusive, you can see why you have so much emptiness inside and why it's so important to create an internal Good Mother relationship now. We stay developmentally arrested at whatever emotional level was achieved when the nurturing stopped or the neglect or abuse took place. There is either the experience of tremendous neediness or going numb to ward off the pain and loneliness.

The ability to comfort yourself, then, comes from appropriate nurturing, and this is precisely why it is so important for survivors to learn to work with their Inner Child. Bonding and separation are two areas that suffer most in an abusive parent-child relationship. These are the two issues that every human being must resolve with his or her parents in order to truly individuate. Successful resolution of these issues means a person has strong internalized Good Mother and Good Father voices that support them both emotionally and in creating successes in the world. Every person needs both of these messages: the unconditional love of "You're perfect just the way you are" (bonding) and the "You can do it" (separation), in order to grow into a whole human being.

Most ACAs and survivors of trauma lack these messages of unconditional love and support. Instead, they have an ongoing inner dialogue of constant criticism; they "beat themselves up" when they're hurting or vulnerable, rather than comforting themselves. Often, they don't even realize they're doing this. When I work with clients on this issue, they are often surprised to learn they have what I call the Critical Voice—surprised because they thought that pattern of thinking was normal. Often ACAs and incest survivors have to be taught exactly what it means to comfort because there is no internal reference point for it: You can't be expected to know what you haven't been taught.

PROCESSES FOR DEVELOPING A NURTURING MOTHER VERSUS A CRITICAL VOICE (HEALING THE INNER CHILD)

The following are some tools and processes to help you recognize your Inner Critic and develop a nurturing parent voice.

Meditation

Get in a comfortable, quiet place where you feel safe. Close your eyes and take a few deep breaths. Allow your body to begin to relax as you watch your thoughts come to the surface. What is worrying you at this moment? What are the issues in your life that are intruding on you right now? Keep allowing the thoughts to bubble up and continue to go deeply inside. Now begin to see a beautiful radiant light pouring down through the crown of your head and moving down through your whole body. Really let go into this light and allow it to soothe away all the tense, achy places in your body. See it moving through your forehead, the backs of your eyes, over your eyebrows, through your neck, down into your shoulders, and on down to your hands. Allow your hands to grow warm and heavy. See the light opening your heart and moving down into your stomach, your pelvis, and on down your legs to your feet, grounding you to the center of the earth.

Now go in your mind to a very safe place—a place that feels sacred and beautiful to you. It might be a meadow with sunlight streaming down and a brook nearby; it might be a mountaintop; it might be your favorite beach. Invite whatever Spiritual Presence feels nurturing to you: It might be your guardian angel, spiritual guides, allies from the animal world, or just a source of energy that's loving and warm.

Now picture a little girl. She might be two years old, or three, four, or five. See her running toward you, smiling. See her innocence, her grace, her playfulness, her charm. See yourself opening up your arms to her, embracing her and allowing her to climb onto your lap. Now allow the Spiritual Presence to bathe both of you in its light. Say to the Child, "I love you and I am here for you. I will always be here for you." Let that sink in for a few minutes. Then slowly bring yourself back to the room. Move your fingers and toes and slowly open your eyes.

Try this type of meditation work as often as you're comfortable—once a day or once a week. You may notice it gets easier to "go inside" with practice, that your "mind chatter" gets quieter and you gradually begin to feel more calm during the day.

Discovering the Critic

Go back to the affirmations with the negative response column, in Chapter Four. Look at your negative responses. This is your Inner Critic.

Again, picture the Child in you. Notice how old she is. What is she is wearing? How is she standing? You may want to find a photograph of yourself as a child and keep it nearby.

Now picture this Child being spoken to by your Critical Voice in the negative response column. If you overheard a real adult screaming these critical messages at a real child, what would you want to do? What would it do to a child to receive these messages? What would you want to say, both to the adult and to the child?

This is where most people hesitate: They don't know how to speak in a nurturing voice in a way that can make contact with the Child. People's responses vary, but typical answers include going over and asking the adult to stop and leave the Child alone, and then picking the Child up. This is a good beginning, but it is also necessary to comfort the Child, to address her directly, to make contact with her. And because the Child is spiritual and emotional, you must speak to her on those terms.

Mother Love Affirmations

If you haven't had sufficient nurturing, you may not have any idea how to connect emotionally or make contact with a child. The following Mother Love Affirmations messages are included here to show you how a nurturing parent might sound when she's comforting a hurting child. Sit down in a quiet place and read through these messages,* noticing which ones speak to you.

I am ready for you; I want you to be alive.
I am here for you; I am right here.

*From *Body, Self and Soul: Sustaining Integration*, by Jack Rosenberg

I love you now and will always love you. Nothing you can do could stop my love for you.

You are beautiful and perfect in my eyes. You are unique in all the world to me.

You are completely lovable just the way you are.

You don't need to do anything to earn my love; I love you just because you are you.

You can trust yourself and your own inner guidance.

I will keep you safe until you can do that for yourself. The world is a safe and loving place and you are always protected.

I will never leave you and it's okay for you to go out into the world and come home again. It's all right for you to have your own life.

You are always connected to love.

If you feel particularly moved by any of these messages, repeat them over and over to yourself. Write them down on a 3 × 5 card and keep it in your wallet so you can pull it out and read them to yourself when you feel lonely or afraid. You also might want to tape these messages to your mirror so that you see them first thing every morning. Look into your own eyes as you're repeating them.

When you are just beginning to develop a nurturing voice, it is useful to put yourself on a Seven-Day Mother Love Affirmations Plan. Write down each of the messages every day for seven days. This will begin to imprint them into your mind. It is necessary to code this voice in, especially if you haven't received such messages from your primary care-givers. Because you've had a lot more practice addressing your Inner Child with the Critical Voice, it will take some practice to learn to speak more gently and for the Child to begin to trust this softer voice. You also may need to evaluate your friends, bosses, and mentors. Do they speak to you in a critical or nurturing voice? Have you replicated your Inner Critic in your relationships? When your Critical Voice is dominant in your own head, it is not unusual for you to have other people around you that talk to you in the same way.

If you keep practicing the Mother Love Affirmations long enough, they will gradually become a natural part of your thinking. Once this happens, it becomes intolerable to allow anyone in your environment to speak abusively to your Inner Child. It no longer feels normal because there is nothing inside you that resonates with the external verbal abuse. This does not mean that it's your fault if there are people around you that are verbally abusive. It just means that now that you're more aware, you've got some choices to make about the environment you're going to put your Child into and how to set boundaries to be more self-protective.

PROCESSES FOR BONDING WITH THE INNER CHILD

How many times do you listen to your Inner Child when she wants to be loved, to play, to notice something beautiful in the world, or when she doesn't like somebody that you continue to sleep with, work for, or otherwise are associated with?

In your mind or on paper, answer the following questions:

Do you know what your Inner Child likes to do?

How do you respond to her when she tells you what she wants, particularly if it is inconvenient or you're rushed?

Do you make time to talk to your Inner Child?

How could you find some time in your life to do that?

This can be an ongoing thought process that you begin to incorporate into your day, or you may design special weekly rituals to teach yourself to notice and remember your Child, before she creates a crisis.

Some possibilities are: visualizing your Child in a car seat next to you while you're driving, or close by when you're in the shower, bath, or on walks. Sitting down with a cup of tea by yourself with a journal, or going to an art museum or a café are good ways to let yourself contemplate and do inner dialogue work with the Child.

Begin to check in with your Inner Child during the day, to say, "How are you doing? What are you wanting?" At first, she may tell you funny or surprising things, like, "I want a hamburger and french fries," even though you don't eat meat, or "I want to go to the zoo," or some other activity that is a fun memory from your childhood that you haven't done in years.

A good technique to use with an unhappy Inner Child is to say, "I promise you a treat if you do this thing that I know you hate. I promise I will restructure our life so that we won't have to do it anymore, very soon."

When rushed you might say, "I am tired right now. I love you but I can't talk right now, but I will hold you." Or "I'll be back in a little while." You may say, "I have to go to work and I'm taking you to the baby-sitter's for the day, but I will come back and we'll do something fun. We can do whatever you want. You can choose."

Then it's very important to follow through and fulfill your promises to her, or tell her no in a gentle and firm way and offer alternatives.

Assessment of Developmental Injuries

To better understand where the injuries occurred for your Inner Child, it's useful to make a history. Get a big piece of posterboard and write notes in different colored magic markers so you can trace the patterns in your childhood and family system. Put all the information about your mother's family in one color, and all the information about your dad's family in another color. Then, with a new color, mark an A for alcoholic beside whichever family member has this disease, through several generations. (See example of genogram on page 165.)

1. How old were your parents when they met, and what was going on in their lives? What are the stories about their courtship? Were there money, work, or family troubles? What were the stresses?

2. What do you know about your mother's and father's families? Was there substance abuse or physical/sexual abuse that you know about? Was there religious or cultural persecution?

3. How long did your parents know each other before they got married? How long after they married were you born? Where are you in birth order among your siblings? How many years are there in between children?

4. Were there any complications in your mother's pregnancy with you? Were there any difficulties in feeding? Were you breast fed or held much as a baby?

5. Was there any substance abuse in your family? Was your mother abusing substances during her pregnancy/ breast feeding of you?

6. What are the stories about you as a child? Are there none? Sometimes the absence of information tells as much as information that exists.

7. Who cared for you during the first five years of your life? Did they want the job?

8. What are your memories of starting school? What was your school performance and your ability to make friends like?

9. What are your memories of adolescence? What are your first sexual memories and experiences? What is the history of your sexual relationships?

10. Were there divorces in the family? Deaths? Suicides? Hospitalizations? Periods when any of the children were separated from the rest of the family?

11. How did you handle any of the above?

12. What is the history of your own substance abuse, if any? What did you abuse and when did you start? If you're in recovery now, how old were you when you got clean?

13. Do you have a history of abusive relationships? When did they occur, and how long did they last?

Now that you know when and where you got hurt as a child, you'll know better where some of the "developmental arrests" may be and what the needs for reparenting will be for the Inner Child. It's just as if you were adopting a child: You'd want to know what her history was so you could be alert to the difficulties she might have with certain issues. For example, if a child has suffered abandonment, she may always be a little sensitive about separations, and feel depressed and/or anxious about disconnecting from others.

Another example is a survivor who didn't get molested during family vacations because the proximity of the other family members kept her safe. As an adult, she becomes anxious and depressed when returning from vacations because there's always that old, familiar feeling of: "Oh no, it's going to start again. It felt so nice to be free and safe for a while and now it's all over." Although she lives many miles away from her perpetrator and has been separated from her family of origin for years, this is her internal dialogue and reaction pattern to a current event. Once she's aware of it, she can be sensitive to herself so that she doesn't spiral down after every trip.

Working with the Inner Child After Losses

Frequently the adult woman in us is ready to leave a relationship before the Inner Child is. Can you imagine having a child who is very attached to a partner in your life and trying to explain to the child that you are going to separate? The most important process is to acknowledge the child's feelings. For example, "I know you're really

---

Example of a genogram:

A = Alcoholism   □ = male

V = Violence   O = female

I = Incest survivor   ◎ = subject

Parents married at ages 17 and 18, to get out of violent, alcoholic homes. Mother–incest survivor. Her father violent; her mother was also a survivor and alcoholic. Lots of deprivation in mother's childhood. Abused by older brother also. Father's father alcoholic; questionable violence—he never talked about his childhood.

Parents knew each other 8 weeks, eloped—families angry. Memories of early marriage—happy but financial problems. First incidence of violence during pregnancy. Difficult birth; no breast-feeding. Father's drinking got worse after 1st child born. Sexual abuse by Dad, beginning at 12. Mom "weak"; unprotective. Constant fights between parents.

School problems. Couldn't concentrate. Few friends. Started acting out and running away at age 13. Chemically dependent by 14. Multiple sexual assaults.

Got sober at 23.

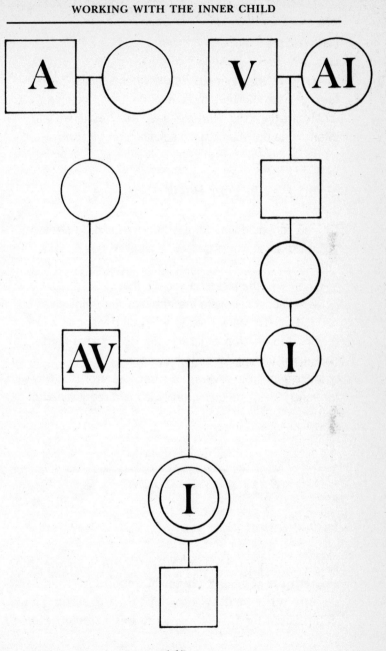

sad. You really hoped we could be with him for a long time. It's okay. I'm here."

Acknowledging our feelings, even the sad and needy feelings, is sometimes more important than doing anything different externally. If we feel seen and heard, we can often come up with creative solutions on our own.

Using Play in Your Healing Process

Do you schedule time to play? If you could do whatever you'd like for a whole day, what would it be? _____

_____

When was the last time you did that? _____

Many incest survivors are afraid to "let themselves go" into their child. Many lived in so much danger as children, they had to develop a "little soldier" complex—hardly conducive training for self-enjoyment.

Make a point to review the "Processes for Bonding with the Inner Child" regularly, until play is a regular part of your day.

CHLOE'S STORY

Introduction

Chloe's story provides another example of the inter-relatedness of incest, chemical dependency, and self-esteem in the healthy growth of the developing child, demonstrating how the incest has affected Chloe's

judgment of healthy partners and made her suscep-
tible to abusive relationships with men. It also portrays
some of the benefits she has gained through her recovery: an empowerment that has allowed her to resume control of her own life, and an ability to accept
and process feelings.

Chloe is an attractive, thirty-seven-year old, divorced white woman, the middle daughter of two
brothers, the younger of whom is retarded. Her mother
is an alcoholic, who drank actively from before Chloe's
birth until Chloe was twenty years old. Chloe's father
is an addict and a drug dealer, recently convicted of
dealing drugs and facing imprisonment. Both parents
were molested as children and come from very dis-
organized homes. Chloe's parents divorced when she
was twelve, and she moved back and forth between
them.

Chloe was molested by her father at least from the
time she was six until she was seventeen. The molestation began with fondling and kissing and led to intercourse when Chloe was twelve or thirteen.

Chloe met her future husband at age seventeen.
When she was eighteen, she and her husband were
involved in a crime. Her husband was sent to prison
for twelve years and Chloe was sentenced to three
years. Chloe did the time and then waited for her
husband. She was very much in love with him, but
after eight years of waiting, she finally gave up.

Chloe abused cocaine and alcohol from the ages of
twenty-three to thirty-one, and has been sober for six
years. She currently runs her own business but has
difficulty feeling motivated to work. She has a strong

sense of lost time—time in which she might have done what she really wanted with her life: to develop as an artist and have children. She feels she is just now learning how to take care of herself, and it is very difficult for her to give up the idea that someday, somehow, she will be taken care of by a man. This is a constant issue in her relationships with men; it also comes up in self-sabotage with money and losing her possessions.

Recovery has meant feeling her emotions, admitting her vulnerability, and being gentle with herself. She is learning to take care of herself, rather than expecting others to do it for her.

Chloe continues to take steps that are empowering to her, and her strong social skills and intellect allow her to get clearer and clearer about what she wants in her life and to create it for herself.

Chloe's Story

My maternal grandmother had thirteen husbands or common-law husbands. One tried to lift my mother's skirt or kiss her, but she pushed him away. My father was abused by his dad, who was an alcoholic. I don't know if my brothers were molested, but I don't think so.

My first incest memories are at six years old or around then. I remember my father thrusting on my thighs and putting my face toward his genitals. The memories are fuzzy: not like whole experiences. I don't remember what happened after that: just feeling distressed. I vaguely remember him saying things like, "This is because I love you, this is a good thing between us, very special." I remember being in my room, freaked out, beyond coping. One more vague memory is of him saying, "Come to my room, Chloe." I don't know if these are all one memory or happened at different times.

I was so afraid to wake up the house or let anybody find out. That explains why it kept happening when I really didn't want it. If I made a scene and woke up the whole house at eleven, twelve, or one at night, everybody would know something was going on. I couldn't make such a huge decision.

Sometimes he'd say, "Well, I'm going to take Chloe to the movies," and then molest me before or after the movie. One time we went to stay with my grandma and aunt, and we slept in the same bed. They weren't suspicious of that. Sometimes it would happen in the day, if my mom wasn't home or something, but mostly at night. My mom was probably passed out drunk. He'd come molest me, then he'd get in the bed with her. He said she was a castrating bitch even though I know she was generous sexually. But that could have been his perception. She is very manipulating and controlling, passive-aggressive. She could have insulted him in their fights. I could picture her that way.

The incest with my father continued on a regular basis until I was almost fourteen. At that time, my parents were divorced and my dad got custody. While he was preparing his boat to go on a long vacation, I got to stay with my mom for a semester of high school. Then my brothers and I went to stay with him on the boat.

I remember asking myself, "Why did I go stay with

him then?" Because I was older and it had stopped temporarily, I thought, "You won't resume it, especially if I indicate that I don't want it. You'll see that I'm a young woman now, not just this little child." It was almost too scary to hope, but deep down I thought, "Oh, good, I'm going to get a father. Now I'll be with Dad, but it won't be sexual." I think that was my hope in traipsing off on a trip with him—that I'd finally have a father after all these years.

Also, it was distressing to stay with my mom. She was drinking real heavy then and her fiancé apparently liked her drunk. It was real sick. She tells me now that I screamed at her, "You're an alcoholic and I hate you. You've got to do something about it." I was the only one who ever said anything flat out. It was really an unhappy time.

So the incest went on from ages six to thirteen regularly, then a few more years—the last one was when I was seventeen. He had intercourse with me after I was thirteen. He broke my hymen and penetrated me for the first time. Then it was intercourse those last few times.

I remember that it hurt. I don't remember him really penetrating me. I remember feeling fear when he was doing it. It was so scary, because it didn't fit; it didn't want to go in; he was pushing. There must have been foreplay for at least ten to fifteen minutes, but I don't remember it like that. I remember pressure. I remember jumping up and being afraid. I remember it seeming bizarre that he was trying to force this thing in there.

We were on his boat and someone came; we heard

him coming down the dock. My dad said, "Go in the head." So I went in the bathroom and I was bleeding. I remember feeling really degraded, that it was so shameful, and that I had to hide it because someone was coming.

Those last few times in my teens were so repulsive. I was so full of hate, I just laid there with this person having sex with him, hating his guts and being resigned.

When I did reject him he was insistent and called me selfish. He was angry and emotionally violent. During this time of living with him on the boat, I had been hanging out with some kids my age, this guy and a girlfriend and her brother. Now as I look back on it, my dad was probably jealous. So he said, "Chloe, come down below," and I knew what that was about. The one time I did stand up to him, I said, "No, I don't want to." He knew that I knew what we were talking about. He said, "Why not? Don't be so selfish." I said, "Dad, I'm fourteen, I'm starting to be a young woman and it really bothers me." He treated me like I was being a selfish little bitch. He yelled, "You get down below!" I thought of jumping in the bay, but I was afraid he'd come in after me; I was afraid of struggling with him in the water. So I did follow him down, and he was a little bit contrite. He said, "Just one more time, baby; I promise you, if you don't like it, if you don't enjoy it, I'll never ask you again," which was a lie, because he not only asked me again, but insisted.

I think that was one of the reasons I remember hating him, bitterly. First of all because it was rape, and then for him trying to make it okay. That was disgusting; I hated him for that. I knew he was counting on making me enjoy it so he could justify it. And then he was forceful the next time and the next time when I said no.

I had tremendously low self-esteem; I felt very soiled, real damaged, dirty, and inferior to all the other little girls—very different. If anybody knew, I'd be abandoned, isolated, very alone, bad. I felt trapped and distrustful; I'm just now starting to uncover the denial system, to make some kind of integrity or cohesion out of life. I know this about kids: They have to believe in their parents, no matter how fucked up they are. Therefore I thought somehow I deserve this shit because he has to know this is what I'm worthy of. This is what I merit. I felt guilt, lots of guilt.

It's stayed the same all my life. I was always intimidated around women; they seemed fresh and worthy and feminine. At baby showers or anything like that, I felt so out of place. The fear kept haunting me that if anybody knew the truth I'd be ostracized, especially by these proper, straight, normal women. I just felt like an outcast. I knew I was less than other people, but they didn't know it. If they did like me it was because they didn't know.

I think that choosing to marry a man who would go to prison and then standing by him were a result of my low self-esteem. I think the incest is part of my disease of being a drug addict.

I had started using pot when I was eighteen and, other than when I was in prison, I used on almost a daily basis for sixteen years. The first time I drank alcohol was when I was twenty-seven and I thought, "Where have I been? What have I been missing?" I felt great, funny, sexy, beautiful, euphoric, and ecstatic. I never had a social drink; I went immediately into daily drinking and daily cocaine use. I was very depressed; I had no skills, no job, no home, and my husband was in prison. When I did the coke I'd talk a lot and feel real connected to other people. I felt like everything I was saying was real important; this resulted in a lot of one-night stands because I thought we were getting so close. I felt suicidal as soon as I came down: I was anxious, nervous, and always felt depressed. I always had to start using and drinking again. My attitude toward the substances was, "Take me out." When other people would start to feel they were getting too high or too numb, they'd want to pull back, but I would just be getting to the place I wanted to be in.

The end result of all this was getting pulled over by the police, having drugs on me when I was still on probation, and freaking out, thinking they were going to send me back to jail. I was court-stipulated to attend meetings, thank God. It was a relief by that point.

In the framework and dynamics of my life, what I have to work with, I still feel the impact of the incest. Even if I give myself some time, keep showing up, am gentle with myself about building my business so I can turn it into a profitable situation in the next few years, I'll be thirty-nine by then and just starting to have a successful business. It's scary being thirty-seven and just beginning. Then I start to feel hopeless. And I'm afraid I'm not going to find a man. It seems like

173

I've been looking for so long and nothing ever works out quite right in my relationships with men. I don't really understand what that's about and if that's connected to the incest and how I feel about my worth and sexuality.

I can't really compare how other women handle those moments of choice-making about whether they're going to sleep with a guy or not. I do know what people from groups and friends have shared with me. I know there have been times when I've probably slept with somebody I didn't know that well because they liked me. Or maybe I knew they didn't care deeply for me, but "They like me, they want me" has been good enough when, in the long run, it wasn't a great choice.

When I have sex, I'm not frigid; I like sex. But I think it's the affection that appeals to me—attention. It's a part of my neediness, that I want someone to want me.

I don't feel like I trance out with a man, but I do feel like there's a level of holding back that occurs that is only broken through sometimes. More rarely, I experience a level of abandonment or relief or undefended vulnerability—but only in some sexual experiences. And in those I cry when I break my defenses. The crying is at how sad all this defense is, how sad it is to have to feel defensive and unsafe. Then to let yourself feel undefensive with somebody just feels so sad. Because of the abuse I couldn't trust; I was hurt and abused and assaulted. It's a happy release to feel able to be open and "there" with my partner in the moment. But at a certain point of undefending, I'll cry and it's okay. One woman in my therapy group said, "How long do I have to cry?" But for me, if my partner feels okay with it, it's okay. I think it startles them, though.

I wonder if someone hasn't been sexually hurt, if they can have vulnerable sex and not have it be partly sad or bitter—sweet, but just be happy and joyful. That feels like an impossibility. That leads me into how I feel about my whole life right now.

Sometimes I want to drop out of therapy and sometimes I want to go two times a week. I just wish it would go faster. My life has been unmanageable for a while. But three or four weeks back, I had this feeling of sadness come up, and I noticed myself going right through it, rather than its turning into depression. It was just like being in the middle of it and knowing it was going to pass and I thought, "This is amazing. Wow! How streamlined." It was really encouraging that maybe this is what it would be like to have feelings instead of being shut down. I mean, life is feelings. This is the objective; this is what I was working for. This is the reward.

Notes on your reactions to Chloe's Story:

How was it for you to read this story? What are you feeling after reading it? At what age did your abuse begin and what forms did it take? How has it affected your choice of partners?

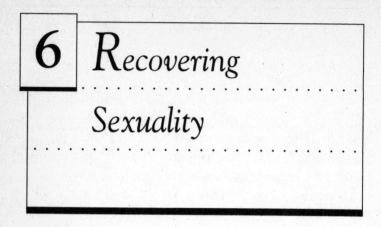

6 Recovering
Sexuality

There's a wonderful analogy to describe the effect of love in our lives. Take a cup of water with mud settled on the bottom and clear water on top. Then begin to pour clean water into the cup. What you'll see first is the water getting muddier as the silt on the bottom is stirred up. Yet if you continue to add water to the cup, the mud will eventually wash out and be replaced by clean water.

This analogy of love's influence is particularly apt in new relationships where you may feel as if all the "mud" is being stirred up. When you begin to be loved by someone, all the parts of you that don't feel lovable seem to rise to the surface—giving you a chance to reexamine them and learn to love them.

It is not uncommon for incest survivors to have very bad feelings about their bodies because of the feelings of shame, confusion, pain, and rage that surrounded their first sexual experiences. Many survivors discover that they feel disdain or disgust for their sexual organs, or are angry at their own sexual response for betraying them if they became aroused during the molestation. Working through negative feelings about your body and learning to love and nurture your physical self can make it easier to develop healthy sexual relationships.

This is one of the most difficult and complex tasks in incest survivor recovery. It is easier, however, once you have begun to process your grief and rage and the nurturing of your emotional self. The point is that it is essential to work through the negative feelings; otherwise, you may find that when you allow someone to get close to you or when you begin to be sexual, that these unresolved feelings return—stirring up the mud at the bottom. This makes for complicated relationships.

> I know that until I process the incest issues, whatever it takes, I'm going to always be affected by the incest for the rest of my life. I have to know that it wasn't my fault and learn how to feel good about myself, which I never did. . . . Then I'll know I have rights, that I can take care of myself, and say no or say yes.
>
> —*from Courtney's Story*

Without processing your feelings, it is easy to remain a victim, responding reactively in relationships and sexual situations. You may not realize the choices you can make: that you can decide whether to be intimate, to set limits, to choose what you want from your partner and a relationship. Once you begin to tune in to your own feelings, heeding what your Inner Child needs, what feelings you feel, you can begin to ask—and answer—important questions about intimate relationships. What kind of relationships am I ready for? Do I want sexual or asexual relationships at this point in my life? Am I ready for a long-term commitment to a partner, or do I want to be with several different partners?

Intimate relationships begin with good feelings about your own body, knowing what you enjoy and what you want. This chapter will describe some of the work involved in nurturing your physical self, your self-esteem, and preparing for intimacy.

RELATIONSHIPS: BOUNDARIES AND SELF-IMAGE

Being aware of your boundaries is the first step toward intimacy. Without adequate boundaries, your identity becomes enmeshed with another's, and there can be no true contact, because there is no sense of self from which to experience the other. Boundaries are different than defenses or "walls" to keep others out. Healthy boundaries are simply a way to know where you end and another person begins.

Without boundaries, intimacy exists as something for which the survivor has no reference point. A survivor's lack of healthy boundaries also leaves her vulnerable to dangerous, self-destructive experiences and relationships. Her low self-esteem, shame, sense of isolation, secrecy, and betrayal interfere with her ability to develop sound judgment about many issues, particularly about choosing partners. Her susceptibility to choosing violent or emotionally unavailable partners increases dramatically.

Most survivors have grown up in families where enmeshment and a lack of intergenerational boundaries have impaired their ability to develop appropriate boundaries. As young children they may have missed the earlier stages of being mirrored (receiving a positive self-image through being looked at, loved, and admired by caretakers), and held (including being held physically and existing in a safe "holding environment"). Without mirroring, children cannot adequately develop an internalized self-image. Not enough holding creates a sense of having no boundaries and an inability to contain feelings. This creates acting-out syndromes in which the survivor is always going "out of control."

Missing an internalized core self, a survivor may attempt to reproduce mirroring through the pattern of the "women who love too much" syndrome—where she gives and gives to a narcissistic partner, and is seemingly oblivious to his faults. This is accompanied by a painful wishing and hoping that if she's just "good enough" and loves well enough, she can get an unresponsive partner to return her love, thereby fulfilling the unresolved childhood need. For these women, this is a repetition of a family pattern: This desperate attempt to be perfect has been the only way

179

to be mirrored, to "be seen," by a parent. Parents of survivors have been narcissistically oblivious to the needs of their children. They have imposed their needs onto the children, so that the child's only hope of feeling connected is to give up her own needs and to adopt a caretaking position.

The other side of the "women who love too much" pattern is the tendency to "escalate" in relationships —to heighten emotional tension and create fights— either because this is the emotional distance that is comfortable or because they believe that closeness is okay only after there's been some pain. Neither pattern contains the possibility for true intimacy, which requires a healthy give and take between the partners.

The repetition compulsion states that when a child has experienced conflicts or traumas in relationships with her parents, she will unconsciously seek out the same personality types in her adult relationships in order to recreate the family situation. This is actually an attempt to replay the conflict in order to work it through, but it can appear as an endless reenactment of the same abusive cycle—in other words, "different partner, same dance." This syndrome is particularly frustrating for survivors who find themselves carrying this pattern of choosing abusive relationships into recovery. However, it is my belief that once a survivor has entered recovery and comes into contact with new information and healthy feedback, this pattern will eventually change, even though it may be one of the slowest to shift.

Although it may look as if the survivor is forever repeating the same mistakes, there is probably some progressive movement. The partners may all be abusive, but the woman may see the pattern and learn to be more honest and self-protective earlier and earlier in each relationship. Eventually there isn't any intrigue or attraction about a potentially abusive or unavailable partner. She has developed the "antennae" to spot the narcissistic personality type, and she can choose to walk the other way before engaging in any interaction.

Breaking out of the addictive relationship cycle requires learning how to establish a core self, to nurture oneself from the inside. When the source of comforting is located inside, it is possible to wean oneself away rather than wrenching away from obsessive relationships. This development of an internal comforter is a task that most people accomplish in adolescence but that survivors often do not accomplish. This process is an extension of the Inner Child work discussed in Chapter Five.

To prepare for intimate relationships or to improve your current relationship, continue the work you have begun on processing your feelings, monitoring what you need, and nurturing your Inner Child. Begin, too, to nurture your body and learn what you need physically. Seek information on sexuality, dysfunctional families, and relationships. Work through the processes throughout this chapter on such issues as boundaries, discovering your feelings about your body, and becoming sexual.

PROCESS FOR DISCOVERING YOUR BOUNDARIES

You can obtain a clearer idea of what and where your boundaries are by performing the following exercise:

With a friend or therapist, sit down opposite one another on a carpeted floor. Take a minute to look at each other and register your feelings: Do you feel comfortable, scared, exposed, curious? Take a piece of chalk and draw a circle around yourself on the carpet to indicate where your boundary is. Draw it whatever size and shape feels right to indicate how much space you need and want around you.

Sit down again and look at your friend. How does that feel? Does it feel any different to be with your friend and have a boundary? Now have your friend draw his or her boundary. How does it feel for both of you to have a boundary? Do you feel safe, guilty, more centered, abandoned? Your feelings will give you information about what messages you received from your family about having your own boundaries.

Now visualize your family in the room with you. What would their boundaries look like? Many dysfunctional families are so enmeshed, their boundaries would be drawn as one big circle around the entire group, or as bombarding circles, overlapping. It is very important to have boundaries to develop a healthy ego and to experience sexual pleasure.

PROCESSES FOR EMOTIONAL INCEST SURVIVORS: CREATING A BOUNDARY

If you have been abused through covert or emotional incest, developing boundaries will be an extremely important issue for you. Covert incest, although less intrusive physically than overt incest, is particularly disturbing because it is so hard to pinpoint and validate exactly what's wrong. One symptom of covert incest is an ongoing sense of being observed whenever you're engaged in sexual activity and/or masturbation and fantasy.

Survivors of this form of abuse often wonder if they're crazy because the family looks so normal to the outside world. Sometimes even in the internal structure of the family it appears that nothing is really wrong. This makes it very hard to legitimize the abuse experience. If you are haunted by a feeling of being observed by the perpetrator, it's very important to construct a way to feel private.

You can do this by using fantasies. Play with the following suggestions or make up your own.

To construct a boundary:

Imagine building a thick wall around the perpetrator.

Imagine putting the perpetrator in a jail or lock-up situation.

Picture the perpetrator tied up.

Picture a very physically strong and powerful being
by your side, ready to protect you from the
perpetrator at any time.

NURTURING YOUR BODY

Because incest is such a violation, all the way down to
your physical boundaries, many survivors have no
connection with their physical bodies. They may see
themselves as only sexual or physical entities or
disassociate from their bodies. Others become obese as a
way of creating a barrier against being sexualized.

Reclaiming your physical self-esteem begins with
learning to nurture your body through good exercise and
diet as conscientiously as you have begun to nurture your
emotional self. It is very important, for example, to include
a manageable exercise program in your recovery process
—to get back in touch with your body and learn to
experience your life from inside it. Any sort of regular
activity can be beneficial: walking, hiking, swimming,
jogging, dancing, biking, aerobics, etc. You can start
gently, by taking a walk once a week and then increasing
the frequency as you build strength and discover the
enjoyment of being in your body—just for yourself. Invite a
friend to go with you or find a regular "exercise buddy."

Begin paying more attention to the foods you eat every
day and how they make you feel. Are you eating mostly
vegetables, fruits, and whole grains—or mostly sugary
and fatty foods? Do you consume much caffeine or
alcohol, or fruit juices and water? Simply by becoming
aware of what your body needs and what helps you feel

good and perform your best can guide you to better nutrition.

If you need more information about good exercise or diet plans, investigate the many sources available: seek out books, look up clinics or specialists, check out programs such as Overeaters Anonymous. The latter is a Twelve Step program for people who are obsessive and compulsive about food, whether or not this is manifested in a weight problem. Overeaters Anonymous will help you focus on which foods set off a compulsion in you (some typical ones are white flour and sugar) and help you keep away from those foods.

Geneen Roth in *Feeding the Hungry Heart* approaches food issues from another perspective. She theorizes that thin people stay thin because they listen to their bodies: They eat whatever they want and stop when they are full. Self-deprivation during dieting, she stresses, will produce bingeing or overcompensating later, while a permissive attitude, along with an exploration of the feelings underneath the hunger, will eventually lead you to a naturally well-balanced diet, in alignment with your own unique needs.

As you learn how to nurture your body through exercise and proper diet, pay attention to the way you feel about your physical body and how you respond to different stimuli.

If you have avoided sexuality for a long time or have always focused on the needs of your partner during sex, it is time to learn how to tune in to yourself. Give yourself some time to expand your range of sensual contact. You may want to begin by increasing your awareness of your sensuality, the pleasure you can feel through all of your senses. What clothing and fabrics feel good to you, close to your skin; what temperatures do you prefer? Experiment with taking baths or putting lotion on your body: Notice how it feels. What smells do you enjoy? What makes your body feel good? What kinds of touch are pleasurable to you?

Learning to distinguish between caring and exploitative touch is very important, along with knowing your triggers (see Chapter One). Note your responses when someone or something touches you. Does that touch make you cringe? Or do you feel warm and safe inside? Do you feel comforted and relaxed or wary and suspicious? What are your emotions—happy, afraid, turned on?

If there is a way that feels comfortable or appropriate to you, it's a very good idea to practice just being touched. You can begin with a small amount of touch, noting your reactions and slowly adjusting to more. You may want to schedule a regular massage with a licensed massage therapist who has some experience or sensitivity in working with survivors, so that he or she can be alerted to what you can tolerate and introduce more kinds of touch gradually. In the beginning, some survivors can allow their massage therapists to touch only their necks and shoulders. It's okay to stay with whatever is comfortable for you now, until you can slowly allow more and more areas to be touched.

PROCESS FOR DISCOVERING YOUR FEELINGS ABOUT YOUR BODY

Get a full-length mirror and stand in front of it, either dressed or, if you can, undressed. Look into your face, into your eyes, and then look at your whole body—every part of it. Be on guard for your Critical Voice and gently replace any negative thoughts with nurturing messages. Continue looking at yourself until you can lovingly accept and praise every part of your body.

Here are a few affirmations on body image to help you in this process:

It's totally safe to be in my body and to be a sexual being.

My body is a source of pleasure to me; there is no shame or pain in me.

I love my body exactly as it is; I love my breasts, my stomach, my hips, my thighs, my legs, my hair and my face. It's the perfect size and shape.

I love my vagina and all the feelings of pleasure my sexual body parts provide me.

I totally trust all the sensations my body brings me.

It's safe for me to feel sexual desire.

I enjoy feeling aroused.

I appreciate all the sounds and smells my body creates when I'm aroused.

I am proud of having a woman's body. It's safe for me to be a beautiful woman.

YOUR SEXUAL SELF

When first confronting their incest issues, some survivors go through a period of feeling a lack of connection with their sexuality. Feeling asexual—without connection to one's sexuality—is an understandable protection against something that has caused so much pain. Because of the incest, feeling sexual can become inextricably linked with danger or terror, particularly because feeling sexual and fearing danger involve similar responses in the central nervous system.

Other survivors may go through periods of wanting to have sex compulsively as a way to feel the adrenaline rush that comes from chasing, conquering, and seducing sexual partners. This is one way survivors avoid the painful feelings of recovery and one reason it is so important to process the negative feelings before expecting to achieve healthy and mature sexual relationships.

Another common tendency is to define oneself as a sexual object and to perpetuate this self-definition in relationships by presenting oneself in a strongly sexual way or rushing into sexuality before any other kind of bonding has developed.

> I can't really compare how other women handle those moments of choice-making about whether they're going to sleep with a guy or not. . . . There have been times when I've probably slept with somebody I didn't know that well because they liked me. Or maybe I knew they didn't care deeply for me, but

"They like me, they want me" has been good enough when, in the long run, it wasn't a great choice.

—from Chloe's Story

Whatever you experience in your own recovery, it helps to acquire accurate information about the female body and sexual response cycle. Many women have never developed any comfortable way to talk about sex, and you may feel shy about asking for information. Women friends can be a great source of information and help to normalize your sexual feelings and experiences. This is especially true for incest survivors, who have usually missed the opportunity many adolescent girls have to talk with friends about their first sexual experiences (their first crush, their first kiss, their first touch).

Begin now to find appropriate places to talk with other women about sexuality and what they experience. Go to workshops (alone or with your partner), talk to your therapist, or participate in a woman's group. Read books about sexuality (particularly masturbation), relationships, and self-esteem. *The New Our Bodies, Ourselves*, by the Boston Women's Health Collective, provides accessible and thorough information about women's bodies and unique health concerns. Nancy Friday's *My Secret Garden*, a collection of women's sexual fantasies, can be a great resource for hearing what other women say about their sexuality.

Even without the additional trauma that incest creates, women in our culture frequently encounter negative images and impressions about their sexuality.

Initiation into sexuality is a very delicate passage in any young woman's life. It may be useful to give yourself some rituals about reclaiming your body for yourself. It's very important to get a lot of support about getting in touch with your own body and sexual organs, including that it is okay to see them and name them.

Give yourself this time to reclaim what was stolen from you. You have a right to experience the pleasure your own body can create, if you want to.

If working with sexual issues seems painful or otherwise unmanageable for you, consider consulting a qualified sex therapist. There are specific techniques that have been developed to work with particular dysfunctions—either in your sexual arousal response or in relationship issues. You may want to try reading and working on some processes on your own. If you still feel blocked, go back to Chapter Two and gather information on therapists specializing in sexual dysfunction. The following is an example of a process designed to increase your awareness of your own sensations. Read through it and follow your own sense of whether it is comfortable for you to experiment with it at this time. Enjoy it if it feels useful to you; if not, proceed, knowing you can return to it any time you want to.

CREATING POSITIVE SEXUAL EXPERIENCES

Get a hand mirror and create a safe time and place for you to spend some time with yourself and your body. Look in the mirror at your genitals and name the parts. Experiment with different kinds of touch, different rhythms of movement, on different parts of your genitals and see what is comfortable and pleasing. Light some candles, have the temperature right in the room, and play some soft, relaxing music. Try out different fantasies to see what is arousing to you. Read Nancy Friday's *My Secret Garden* for an idea of other women's sexual fantasies.

Remind yourself that your current experience of your sexuality is different from your past experience.

DISCOVERING WHAT YOU WANT

Recovery is learning to make choices instead of responding reactively. How do you feel about being sexual in recovery? What are your fears? If you're not presently involved in a sexual relationship, when would you like to be? What qualities are you looking for in a partner? What makes you feel safe and what makes you feel unsafe? If you could have exactly what you wanted, what would your next sexual encounter be: Describe it to yourself from beginning to end. Do you want the freedom to explore multiple partners? Do you prefer casual sex? A committed relationship? A friendship that becomes sexual over time? Dating experiences that are mildly sexual? Some combination of the above?

By being patient with yourself and listening, you can discover your own answers to these questions. Only you know what it is you feel, what you need. Your responses to these questions will be unique to you, just as your recovery is unique. The recovering stories shared in this book should give you some idea of how personal each woman's experience is. Each of these survivors has answered these questions in a different way.

How to Take Care of Yourself if You Don't Want to Be Sexual

Some women in recovery choose sexual abstinence for a period of time in order to develop a relationship with themselves separate from their sexuality. Because of the incest, you may not have had a chance to develop a personal identity apart from your sexual identity. The reparenting task is to give your Inner Child time to be a child and not sexualize her.

Once you feel more ready to enter into an adult relationship, questions that arise are: "How do I know if I want to be sexual?" "What do I like?" "What don't I like?" "What if I want to be close to someone emotionally or physically but don't want to be sexual?" "How do I set limits?" Learning to read your internal cues involves asking yourself continually: "What do I want?" "What do I need?" Be specific. Write down the answers until you can say them out loud.

These are excellent questions to talk over with a therapist or women friends, who might be able to share their thoughts and experiences with limit-setting and vulnerability.

How to Take Care of Yourself When You Do Want to Be Sexual

When you are ready for sexual intimacy it will be with a new sense of choice and an awareness of your own needs. The following is a bill of sexual rights developed by Wendy Maltz and Beverly Holman. (Their book, *Incest and Sexuality*, is an excellent source for further information about this stage of recovery.) Go over this list point by point, noticing whether any of the rights bring up your Critical Voice, seem difficult to accept, or seem foreign to your own beliefs. You may want to read this list each day for seven days, or write it down for yourself to code it into your thinking.

Bill of Sexual Rights

I have a right to own my own body.

I have a right to my own feelings, beliefs, opinions, and perceptions.

I have a right to trust my own values about sexual contact.

I have a right to set my own sexual limits.

I have a right to say no.

I have a right to say yes.

I have a right to experience sexual pleasure.

I have a right to be sexually assertive.

I have a right to be the initiator in a sexual relationship.

I have a right to be in control of my sexual experience.

I have a right to have a loving partner.

I have a right to have sexual preferences.

I have a right to have a partner who respects me, understands me, and is willing to communicate with me.

I have a right to talk to my partner about the incest.

I have a right to ask questions.

I have a right to receive accurate sexual information.

I would add, "I have a right to stop a sexual interaction at any time during it if I begin to feel uncomfortable."

Reclaiming your sexuality does not come all at once. You may continue to feel the effects of the incest even as you experience sexual relationships. The experience, however, does not need to be threatening or painful.

> When I have sex, I'm not frigid. . . . I don't feel like I trance out with a man, but I do feel like there's a level of holding back that occurs that is only broken through sometimes. More rarely, I experience a level of

abandonment or relief or undefended vulnerability—but only in some sexual experiences. And in those I cry when I break my defenses. The crying is at how sad all this defense is, how sad it is to have to feel defensive and unsafe. Then to let yourself feel undefensive with somebody just feels so sad. Because of the abuse I couldn't trust; I was hurt and abused and assaulted. It's a happy release to feel able to be open and "there" with my partner in the moment. But at a certain point of undefending, I'll cry and it's okay.

—from Chloe's Story

Once You Become Sexual

Notice what it's like to for you when you get aroused, respond sexually, with orgasm, when you feel satisfied and good during and after sex. When you are aroused, do you feel turned on? Happy? Afraid? Does being sexual bring up feelings of being "dirty"? How do you feel about your own orgasms? Do they ever make you cry?

What is your favorite sexual experience? What is your favorite fantasy, the perfect scenario? What is your favorite time of day or night for lovemaking?

Can you let yourself be present with your partner during sex? Do you feel like you're outside of your body, watching yourself? How do you feel about kissing? Can you let yourself become aroused? Are there any parts of your body you don't like having touched? Is it okay to have a light on during sex? Do you prefer it to be dark? Do you have a lack of sexual desire because you associate sexual feelings with the abuse?

Do you have any pain during intercourse? Is there any difficulty during lovemaking, emotionally or physically? Do you experience a lack of pleasure by placing primary importance on your partner and his or her pleasure? Do you ever enjoy sex and then punish yourself afterward?

Pain during intercourse or a lack of orgasm in masturbation or with a partner may have a physical origin. When was the last time you had a gynecological exam?

For many women, going to a doctor is very traumatic. Do you have any fears about having a pelvic exam? Do you avoid going to the gynecologist? If you need to go, would you find it easier if a friend went with you? Would you find it easier to see a woman doctor rather than a man?

Abortions

Efforts to be present in your body and to experience sexuality may bring up memories or feelings about past abortions. You will need to examine and work through these emotions, as you did with feelings of grief and rage. What abortion experiences did you have? How old were you and what were the circumstances? Did you want the abortion or were you in conflict? Did anyone go with you to the procedure? Was there anyone to talk to before and after? Do you have any guilt, anger, or grief about an abortion that needs to be recognized? Specifically, do you have anger at parents or partners for their participation or lack of participation?

If you have residual feelings, write about your memories and share them with someone. If there is grief about not carrying the pregnancy to term, allow yourself to grieve. You may even want to create some observance or ritual, giving yourself a chance to mark the event. One survivor bought two balloons and went out to a place overlooking the ocean. There she let the balloons go: one balloon for the child that might have been and the other for herself—to forgive herself and let herself be free.

Being with Your Partner: Relationship Skills

If you are in a relationship, it will become important at some point to learn how to make requests of your partner. You may find this a particularly difficult skill to learn, but it is a skill like any other that can be acquired with practice. Often people expect that somehow their partner can just guess what they want. They may even take this notion a step further and believe that their partner's ability to guess their needs is a sign of their love. Or they hope that by giving their partner whatever it is that they like, their partner will telepathically understand what they are asking for. Unfortunately, this form of magical thinking usually results in resentment, frustration, and disappointment. You need to take responsibility for learning to tell your partner your sexual preferences, moment to moment. Then ask your partner what she or he is willing to do? What is she or he able to do? Ask yourself what choices you have, if your partner can't meet your needs.

Respecting Limits

As you become aware of your needs and develop the skills to communicate them, the next step essential to a mature, loving relationship is the ability to respect your partner's limits. In all relationships, no matter how loving, there will be times when you ask your partner for something and he or she tells you no. This can be very difficult, especially if you've had to work hard to give yourself permission to want something and ask for it. You may experience humiliation, shame, or anger. You may be tempted to shut down, to protect yourself from the feelings of disappointment and rejection. You may want to revert back to a position of "I don't need anything from anybody."

It requires a great deal of tenderness and patience to weather the disappointment, to honor your feelings, nurture your Inner Child, and choose to stay open and love your partner with his or her limitations. The needy Child in you may feel "all or nothing" about your relationship. She may need to have a temper tantrum or cry, but if you can keep loving her, you can move back into your adult.

The adult part of you has the capacity to see that

disappointment is normal and expectable in any relationship. It does not mean that you are not loved. Maybe it's your turn to give. Knowing when to bend and when to stand firm is an art. Knowing how to lose gracefully is a sign of maturity and dignity.

PROCESS FOR LONG-TERM RELATIONSHIP UPKEEP SKILLS

Long-term relationships require ongoing evaluation. Monitor your needs and emotions by periodically asking yourself the following questions. Be specific and write down the answers to these questions below or in a journal or other private place that you can come back to later on.

What does it mean for you to feel loved?

_____

_____

What does it take for you to feel loved?

_____

_____

What are you asking for?

_____

_____

199

Make requests of your friend or partner. Listen to the answer to your request. Is your partner willing and/or able to respond to your request? If the answer is yes, you have a mutual goal. If the answer is no, decide on your choices:

Can you get the need met somewhere else?

_____

_____

Can you compromise/live without the need being met and accept the limitations of your friend and the relationship?

_____

_____

These issues are discussed further in *Stage II Relationships*, by Earnie Larsen.

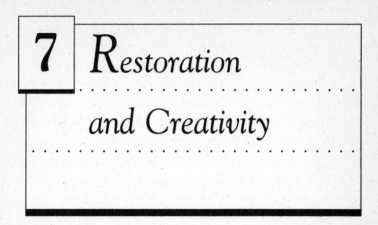

7 | Restoration

and Creativity

At this point you may be asking, "Am I ever going to feel ready to get on with my life? Is there anything to look forward to after the feelings and the pain?"

The answer, unequivocally, is "Yes!"

Because of the work you've done with the earlier phases of your recovery—from breaking denial and seeking help, to working with your feelings and your Inner Child, to recovering your physical self—something within will begin to say, "I am done with the most intense period of grieving and raging. These feelings may return but they will probably be softer. The abuse happened to me. It was not my fault and it wasn't fair. It unalterably changed my life. I wish it hadn't happened, but maybe I can create something useful from the experience. I am ready to move forward now."

While the process of recovery is never over, an important shift occurs that allows you to transform your

injuries into assets, your vulnerability into strength.
Through the grieving, raging, and Inner Child work,
you have begun the process of restructuring your past.
This opens the way for you to begin creating the life
you really want, in the present and for the future. It
is indeed possible to get on with your life, but more
fully and more creatively for having been in recovery.

> Three or four weeks back, I had this feeling
> of sadness come up, and I noticed myself
> going right through it, rather than its turn-
> ing into depression. It was just like being in
> the middle of it and knowing it was going to
> pass and I thought, "This is amazing. Wow!
> How streamlined." It was really encouraging
> that maybe this is what it would be like to
> have feelings instead of being shut down. I
> mean, life is feelings. This is the objective;
> this is what I was working for. This is the
> reward.
>
> —*from Chloe's Story*

This change comes from a newly integrated sense
of self: You know what you know and feel what you
feel. There are no more secrets. There is no more
denial. You can have your privacy without keeping
secrets that are destructive to intimacy; you don't have
to be in denial of any kind. You can make choices.
You have boundaries. You know that every relationship has limits and you know your own. You are no
longer reactive but instead can act from your own

center. You have the capacity to respond and be responsible for your feelings, your relationships, and your life.

There is more work to do in transferring the raw feelings into strength, synthesizing new meanings from the knowledge you have gained. The restoration phase of recovery includes *acceptance*, or coming to terms with the past; *reorganization*, or aligning your present priorities and environment with your new outlook on life; and the *reawakening* of your creative and spiritual faculties.

ACCEPTANCE—REFRAMING THE PAST

In acceptance you will complete the working through and reframing of past events so that you're no longer haunted by them. You can let them go and move on. You may find there is more rage work to be done, and more grieving. The difference now is that your rage and your grief are more focused.

One of the most powerful ways to reframe the past is through forgiveness. This includes forgiveness of yourself and your Inner Child, along with her feelings of guilt or confusion about complying with the incest, and all of her fantasy material as well. It also means forgiveness of others: your siblings, mother, father, extended family, teachers, friends, the men in your life, therapists. For some survivors, it will include forgiveness of the perpetrator.

Opinion is sharply divided about forgiveness of incest perpetrators. Some people object to forgiving perpetrators and maintain that only a sick society allows men to abuse their power. Forgiveness, they feel, is in some way condoning incest. They view survivors' anger as necessary and even beneficial in carrying on the fight to create change, both through political action and public awareness.

For others, incest begins to look like a cycle of abuse passed down from generation to generation with the perpetrator usually being a victim himself. At this point, forgiveness is a very important part of the process of letting go so that survivors can reclaim their own personal power. You may never like the perpetrator or the act but you can have a sense of being free of its negative energy. It's always a good idea to do forgiveness work knowing that it is for yourself, for your own freedom and release.

Be aware that forgiving the perpetrator is a very powerful step, and one that you should work through with a therapist, sponsor, or good friend. (See the "Forgiveness Exercise" later in this chapter.)

Another aspect of acceptance is the ability to think paradoxically rather than in black-and-white terms. This means that instead of saying, "Incest was a bad thing in my life; my life was made bad by it," you are able to accept both the good and the bad that have come from it: "These bad things happened and this is the good I can create from them." Or "These are the bad experiences I had with my family, and I did have this one experience that I really value."

As you come closer to acceptance you will begin to

feel more complete about your past, and ready to put it behind you. Gradually your focus will shift to the present, and you will want to begin a reorganization of your life.

REORGANIZATION—TAKING CARE OF THE PRESENT

Reorganization is signaled by having more energy for current events, and wanting to make changes emotionally, spiritually, and physically. In making these changes you will recognize the need to organize, problem-solve, and establish priorities in your life. These are "adult functions" that require logic and patience, two attributes people in perpetual crisis may not have acquired. This is why people from dysfunctional backgrounds tend to stay in crisis, and people with stable backgrounds tend to create stable lives. As a survivor, you need to know that stability can be learned, and that it will lead the way to expansion and lasting, positive change in your life.

Reorganization may begin with a desire to organize your environment. You may find yourself cleaning out closets, throwing away old clothes, and cleaning out your car, purse, or address book. Suddenly you may be setting up a filing system, keeping a calendar, weeding through the piles of things in your house and folding them away in baskets or boxes. Your recovery work up to this point has been about cleaning house, emotionally and spiritually, discarding the old burdens you've been carrying around for too long. Now you are ready to carry out this clearing and releasing in your physical environment as well.

Creating order is the first step in living a creative life. It is the essential nurturing ingredient and the foundation for having a successful life in which your dreams can come true and you can reach your goals. It is an external manifestation of self-esteem. Are you willing to have an ordered life? What happens to your "inner teenager" and your "rebel"? How have you romanticized your chaos? How have you dressed it up or believed that it's what makes you free, interesting, artistic, eccentric, original, different from the establishment, or from all those other poor souls who "bought into the system"? How do you feel about yourself when things are calm and ordered in your life? Order and organization are elements that most people from crisis backgrounds either never learned or feel great avoidance for. "Terminal vagueness" is a Debtors Anonymous term that describes many abuse survivors' attitudes toward their time and money.

Assistance in these areas is plentiful and easily accessible. Many people find it helpful to consult a time management expert or to hire a professional organizer to help them set up systems to keep track of daily events and commitments.

Debtors Anonymous is a Twelve Step organization that teaches you not only how to manage your money but also to look at the underlying issues of low self-esteem, shame, belief in deprivation, and fear of success that perpetuate a debtor lifestyle.

Other resources include college courses and one-day workshops you can take to learn practical life skills such as how to balance your checkbook or how to budget your time and money. Books you may want to consult include *Prospering Woman*, by Ruth Ross, *Dynamic Laws of Prosperity*, by Catherine Ponder, and *Getting Organized*, by Stephanie Winston.

Problem-Solving

ACA and incest families don't deal effectively with problem-solving. They operate in denial, or by escalating, or they become paralyzed and immobilized. If these are your models, you will probably re-create them in your own life until you seek out new models and learn new skills.

Problems do not have to seem overwhelming or unfair. They are a natural part of life and sometimes even an interesting challenge. Recovering people often struggle with the idea that there aren't supposed to be problems. If you were chemically dependent, you used substances to make all your problems go away. In sobriety, you may feel shocked to find out that just because you're staying clean, everything doesn't immediately "become all right." There's a feeling of "I'm doing the right thing now; this problem isn't supposed to be happening to me."

If you're an ACA, you may have the feeling that you have already given more energy than your fair share to solving problems, and now it's somebody else's turn to take care of you, once you've finally admitted to how needy you really feel.

The reality of life is that all adults have to deal with problems and a certain amount of life is about problem-solving. As M. Scott Peck says in his book *The Road Less Traveled*, "Life is difficult." It doesn't mean you did something wrong. Even people who have had their dependency needs met still have "existential problems": how to create meaning and pleasure in their lives or resolve such issues as loneliness and relationships, as well as the general upkeep of life. You have to learn to build in a margin for error in yourself and others. Sometimes you have to make decisions without enough information. Things break down, disappointments occur, life has limitations, and there are expectable losses. These are harder to absorb when they hit on top of earlier, unexpected losses. But you don't have to succumb to despair or feel as if it's a personal affront every time a problem arises.

You may always be a little sensitive around losses, separations, anger, and your memory triggers, but as you move through recovery, you can expect less and less emotional charge to be attached. All you can do is your best, knowing you will learn as you live through more experiences and take some healthy risks.

Restoration—Creating the Future

As you complete acceptance and reorganization, you may have a sense of feeling more whole. You will probably notice that it is easier to get things accomplished. You feel more fully yourself, as if you've been restored to the level of functioning you might have achieved without the detour of the addictions and/or abuse.

With your physical environment more ordered, and your emotional self more stabilized, you can begin to develop in spiritual ways to complete your healing process. Your life may always include circling back into the feelings of pain and rage, but there can be a sense of reaching deeper and deeper levels of feeling, "unpeeling the onion." Survivors frequently find that feelings get softer, mixed with a bitter-sweet or philosophical feeling. There is no end to incest survivor recovery. It is never "over." But there is an increasing sense of being empowered.

> There are times when I'm quite numb to the past and then there are other times when it hits me in that soft and vulnerable place and there's a great deal of sadness. Sometimes, it also produces a great deal of anger. At this point in my recovery, though, after I feel the feelings and let them pass through me, I almost always move to a deeper level of understanding.
>
> *—from Isadora's Story*

Begin your spiritual opening with the Higher Power of your Twelve Step work, if you have one. If something is troubling you, or you have other issues in your life that you have questions about but no one to consult with about them, write a letter to your Higher Power. Tell Him/Her/It everything that's going on.

Imagine a conversation between yourself and your Higher Power, as if you were sitting face to face. How would your Higher Power respond to you? What would your Higher Power say about the problem?

Then write a letter back to yourself, starting with, "Dear Child . . ." Many people are amazed at the information they receive from this process.

CREATIVITY, DETERMINATION, AND PURPOSE

With acceptance and recognition, you may feel less of an "empty hole" inside. In its place you may sense a restless feeling, a creative urge. Discovering what brings moments of creative inspiration and making time for them in your daily life is a very important part of self-love and of integration of the pain of the past—*and* moving beyond it. The highest end result of pain and grief is to channel them into creativity.

Everyone is creative once they're in a state of self-love. Once you have discovered the wellspring of your creativity, it only gets stronger and stronger. It is the nature of life to be always expanding and progressing into a higher level of order.

Creativity has been described by Dr. Jim Munson, a Science of Mind minister, as a "profound welling up, where the whole Universe is trying to escape from your being into expression." True creativity is almost always experienced as a "high" or a peak experience and usually also as a feeling of calm and great joy.

Psychologist Abraham Maslow found that during peak experiences individuals have a variety of sensations. He listed them as: wholeness; simplicity; perfection; just-right-ness; completeness; fulfillment; aliveness; spontaneity; full-functioning; richness; differentiation, complexity, intricacy; honesty; nakedness; beauty; goodness; uniqueness; effortlessness; lack of strain, striving, or difficulty; grace; playfulness; fun; joy; amusement; gaiety; humor; exuberance; pure, clean autonomy and independence; self-determination; environment-transcendence. (*Toward a Psychology of Being*, pp. 74–83.)

Notice when you have moments at which you feel any of these qualities. Then ask yourself, what was going on right before it? Were you exercising, expressing your feelings, spending time with a particular person, saying a prayer, or working at something creative? You may be so accustomed to struggling to survive or waiting for something negative to happen that you need to train yourself to notice your joy.

Use your experience as a well from which to draw creative ideas. You have a message that no one else does. You have achieved a degree of expertise in an uncharted territory. You don't have to be a public speaker to share your story. Write it down in a story, a book, a song, a play. Submit it to a magazine, or bind it and share it with a few treasured friends. AA says, "Give it away to keep it." Sometimes a recovering person doesn't see how far she's come in her own personal growth until she is talking to another survivor who's at an earlier point in her recovery.

Let the pain come out through drawing pictures or simply playing with the colors of paints or pastel chalks (see Chapter Four). What shape are your feelings today? What color are they? Put down splashes of paint without trying to make forms. Draw a series of pictures or paintings over a period of time to track your healing. Notice the changes. What does it feel like to use black paint, red paint, pink and yellow? Does your choice of color in your clothes or home reflect a particular habitual feeling?

Can you use colors to influence your moods for yourself or to consciously send a message about yourself to others? How do people respond to you when you're wearing all black, navy, or brown, rather than red or yellow? As you stay in recovery, do you notice you are becoming attracted to new colors? Try on clothes in different colors than those you're used to, even if you're shopping at a thrift store or just buying a scarf, a ribbon, or a pair of socks.

Take little risks, but take one every day to open yourself up to something new. This leads to empowerment and mastery.

Finally, use your rage to fuel your determination. Let it push you from behind or from within to get up and do what you need to do in the world. Define your purpose. Write it down and keep it with you. What do you want to do in this life before you leave? If you knew you only had one more month to live, what would you do with it? Where do you want to go, what do you want to see, to whom do you need to speak? What do you want your life to say about who you are? How would you want to be remembered? Write your epitaph.

How do you define the meaning of your life? How do you want to change the world? Who are your mentors? Who inspires you? Read their life stories and study how they raised themselves up. Don't give up before the miracle! When you are feeling low, where can you draw your inspiration from? What piece of music or literature or person renews you?

We must use the suffering to create meaning and vision and purpose. The rage can be the source of stamina. With creativity and determination, there is nothing you can't do.

ABOUT "SLIPS"

This is a term borrowed from Alcoholics Anonymous about alcoholics who resume drinking after being abstinent for some time. All people in recovery are vulnerable to "slips" into old behavior: acting the victim, numbing out, acting out, forgetting to take care of the Inner Child, and so on. You have many new skills to learn and old patterns to change. Forgive yourself if you find yourself in a slip; this is natural. You are on the road to recovery.

FORGIVENESS EXERCISE

Begin your forgiveness work with meditations. Visualize white (or pink) light all around you, and then see it surrounding any person or situation that needs your forgiveness. See a band of it running from your heart to another's.

If you have trouble with the idea of forgiveness, back up

and do more rage work. Write "rage letters" that you may or may not choose to send when you're done. If you decide to mail them, you may want to run them by someone first. Or the process of writing may be enough. Write to everyone you feel anger toward, stating, "This is what you did to me." Be specific, and then tell them, "This is how it made me feel."

When your rage letters are done, write "forgiveness letters" to everyone you've had negative feelings toward:

All the men in your life

Every friend you ever had

Your siblings

Your mother and father

Your extended family

Your teachers, nuns, therapists

The perpetrator

Love Is Letting Go of Fear, by Gerry Jampolski, is a good reference on forgiveness work.

PROCESSES FOR DEVELOPING PROBLEM-SOLVING SKILLS

Think of the one problem that's bothering you most right now. It might be wanting to make more money or wishing you were in a relationship. Define it as clearly as you can. Then run it through the following stages:

Process Your Feelings

It's impossible to do creative problem-solving when you're overwhelmed with feelings about the problem. Unprocessed feelings will drain your energy, and distort and limit your perceptions about new possibilities. For example, do you feel angry, sad, lonely, or upset about a lack of money or relationship? Are you blaming yourself, are you angry at God or others? The first step in problem-solving is always to express and release feelings until you're feeling as light and free as possible.

Take Stock

Take a good look at the problem. Problems can be viewed as parts of a puzzle, to be taken apart and put back together. What is the matter and what is the extent of the loss or damage? What is your estimate of what it will take to fix it? For example, maybe you need a certain amount of money. Define the amount and state the date you want it by. Then break the amount down into incremental chunks; for example, $1200 in a year means you want an extra $100 a month. Breaking this problem further into parts would entail deciding: What do I need to change to make that happen? Some choices are:

Where can I spend less?

How can I earn more money at my current work?

Is there some alternate way to create more income?

Could I take on some extra work temporarily?

What would I gain or lose by doing so?

What are all my options?

Sometimes through this sorting out, we discover new ways of doing things that are better than what existed before.

Research the Problem

Most problems result from either not having enough information or not having enough support.

1. *Get more information—ask questions.*

You can't be expected to know what to do about a problem if you've never had any experience with it before. You weren't born knowing how to write resumes, sign up for a class, or join a gym, let alone knowing what good nutrition is or how to manage money and time. These are tasks that healthy, organized families teach their children and allow them to practice over a five- to ten-year period before they send them out into the world.

One of the most frustrating experiences in recovery is being constantly confronted with problems and life issues that are age-appropriate but that you've had no preparation for because of years of addiction or your upbringing in a dysfunctional family. While other people were developing frustration tolerance in adolescence, most addicts were running wild, continuing to think they were

216

invincible and that rules were there only for other people. ACAs were being "little soldier adults" or "little professors" when other kids were learning how to play and have fun. So there is a constant feeling of "catch-up," and often a feeling of embarrassment when life expects you to know something that you are completely blank on. It's like suddenly being transferred from the fifth to the twelfth grade with no tutoring in between. So you need tutors now, probably lots of them.

One of the best research techniques is to find someone who's gone through this exact problem before and to ask them questions. Who do you know who knows something about the problem you're facing? Ask to talk with them and "pick their brain." If they can't help you, ask them if they know anybody else who could supply you with more information. Most people love to be called on for specific advice. It's nice to be considered an expert on something.

2. *Get more support—ask for help.*

When you're facing a new challenge, you need a lot of emotional support. It's scary and you always feel a little off-center until a problem is resolved or at least until you have an action plan. Let someone know what you're going through and ask them for support during this time.

3. *Break the problem down into manageable pieces.*

Can you separate out issues that are tangled together? What is their order of importance? What needs to be handled first? Is there any danger to you if you don't handle something? Do you need to handle one piece of the problem first so you'll have more information about another piece? Are there any externally imposed time deadlines you need to pay attention to? Is it possible to meet them? Can you negotiate for more time by making a phone call or writing a letter? It's very difficult to come up with creative solutions if you're so pressured that you are feeling overwhelmed, but sometimes having a deadline or cut-off point can lend an energizing edge that helps to get the job done.

4. *Make an action plan.*

Write a list of the actions you need to take. Then break the action plan into even smaller steps, making sure they are manageable and feasible. Next to each action step, write down the date by which you want to complete it. It may be helpful at this point to make up a big three- or six-month calendar on a poster board to get an overview of your time. What do you want to accomplish in the next three to six months? How about one month, one week, and one day? This will allow you to map out your course and know where you stand at any given time. It's okay to revise your dates, but it's a good idea to begin with something concrete so you can get started.

Remember the Serenity Prayer

The Serenity Prayer is "God, grant me the serenity to accept the things I cannot change, the courage to change the things I can, and the wisdom to know the difference."

What about this particular problem can't be changed and just needs to be accepted? What about it can be changed? Is there action that you could take but that you're afraid of? What about it requires courage? What are you willing and able to do? By when?

Brainstorm/Visualize

If you could have the exact outcome you want, what would it be? The following is a brainstorming exercise:

Get a big piece of poster board, lots of colored pens, and an egg timer. Set the timer for two minutes and let yourself think about the problem for that amount of time. Then set the timer for another two minutes and write down on the poster board every idea for a solution that comes into your head, no matter how crazy or unrealistic it seems. Be silly and outrageous.

If you can't think of any solutions, keep writing, "The perfect solution for this situation comes to me now," over and over. This is a great process to do with a friend or a group because other people's minds won't impose the same limitations on a problem that you do when it's a personal issue.

CREATIVE VISUALIZATION

About the past: If you could restructure your childhood or give your Inner Child the ideal childhood, what would it be like? Begin to ask yourself: If I could have any kind of childhood, what would I have given myself?

About the present: If I could have the kind of life I want now, what would it be? What would I do for fun? What would my social life be? What would I do for my creative endeavor? What kind of a home would I have? Where would I go on vacation? What does my Inner Child want? What does my "teenager" want? What does the adult woman in me want? Are they compatible? Can I combine aspects so everybody gets what they want? Take time to visualize your ideal life.

About the future: Go for your dreams, one day at a time. Write out what you'd like. Make an action plan. Put time frames on them. Break big projects down into very small steps. If you get stuck, backtrack and make the action step smaller.

Make small commitments to yourself or to a friend. Follow through with "check-ins." Describe how you met or didn't meet your commitment; receive praise for meeting it or help deciding what blocked you (maybe you really didn't want to do it at all). If you decide you don't really want something, scratch it off your list so you feel complete. Incomplete projects and goals drain your energy on some level. If you find that you want to have it eventually but not right away, give it a new date, further in the future, and put it on your "long-term goals" list. If you still want the goal and are willing to do something about it now, recommit and start again.

POSITIVE FEEDBACK LOOP

PERSISTENCE BUILDS DISCIPLINE.

DISCIPLINE + PASSION = RESULTS.

RESULTS BUILD TRUST, SELF-CONFIDENCE, AND SELF-ESTEEM.

SELF-ESTEEM YIELDS RESULTS.

You can see how this is a positive feedback loop. Once you enter it, results are easier to achieve. This may be why some people seem to be successful at everything they try and others seem to be stuck in losing cycles that never seem to break. Or at times someone continually nears success but something terrible always happens to prevent it.

Some people believe that our thoughts have an influence on our lives—that positive thinking brings about positive outcomes, while negative thinking brings about negative outcomes. What sorts of thoughts do you habitually entertain about your own abilities to realize your dreams or create the life you want? Are you listening to your Critical Voice or can you enter the positive feedback loop?

Two books, *Sermon on the Mount*, by Emmett Fox, and Ernest Holmes's *The Science of Mind*, are excellent references on these metaphysical concepts.

EPILOGUE: THE DESTINATION

You have traveled a long way now. You know the terrain of your recovery journey—the light and dark places. You know that both light and dark places are necessary and that you can survive both the joy and the pain. Keep moving up to higher ground. You may continue to cycle through the phases of memory recall, grief, anger, and sexuality as new events in your life test your strengths in these areas. But the dark places have hope now because you've lived through them; nobody can give you that experience or take it away from you. Certain Native American groups teach that those in the tribe who've faced a death of some kind—emotional, physical, or spiritual—become the shamans for the rest of the community because of the wisdom and courage this experience has earned them. You are a pioneer and a scout, through exploring this territory that has been a secret until now. You are a victor because you have fought a battle with unseen demons. Your victory is a new sense of self and a realization of having reclaimed your life and your heart.

A Note to Partners of Survivors

If your partner is a survivor of childhood sexual abuse, you have probably felt a bewildering array of emotions. Typical responses are confusion, anger, guilt, pain, frustration, and compassion. These feelings are a natural reaction to loss or trauma. Making the discovery that your partner is an incest survivor is a loss for both of you. That is why the succession of feelings outlined above are similar to the stages of grieving Elisabeth Kübler-Ross describes in her book *On Death and Dying*: denial, anger, bargaining, depression, and acceptance.

It is possible to move through these feelings and on to hope and healing. First, however, it's important to become as knowledgeable as you can about the issue of incest, and give yourself permission to have all your feelings. Then you can begin to explore the recovery process and what *you* need for yourself during each stage.

As outlined in the book, each survivor's recovery process is individual but will roughly follow a series of expectable stages. These are: 1) identifying the incest and defining oneself as a survivor, which may require breaking denial; 2) grieving and feeling the pain; 3) expressing rage—a healthy reaction to loss; 4) learning how to nurture the lost child; 5) recovering a healthy sense of sexuality; and 6) discovering joy, spirituality, and creativity.

As traumatic as the discovery of and recovery from incest is for a couple, it is possible to use it to grow closer to each other. Recovery demands a level of emotional honesty and communication that can actually add to the health of a couple. It can be the impetus for a spiritual search that brings greater depth and joy than was available before breaking denial. But it requires hard work. You will have to practice new tools and weather many emotional storms.

WHAT TO EXPECT

Confusion and Guilt

If your partner hasn't verbally identified herself as a survivor yet, the first reaction you may experience is a vague feeling that something is not quite right. Some of the more obvious clues that your partner may be a survivor are: periods of amnesia for portions of her childhood; "splitting off" from her body, particularly during sex; and "startle response."

"Splitting off" means your partner gets blank or

goes numb; she's with you physically, but not internally present. It's as if your partner has left her body and is watching herself have an experience, not internally experiencing it. Some survivors describe their splitting off as floating above themselves and looking down at a situation; others feel like they can make themselves very small, an invisible observer. This is a survival mechanism for all survivors of trauma. It is now probably not in her conscious control. She has had to train herself to "go away" inside to survive unacceptable circumstances. Any current experience that resembles the trauma will either begin to trigger a memory or she'll unconsciously split off to avoid this. This is the reason splitting off occurs so often during sexual experiences.

If your partner "split off" often enough during her childhood, there may be many experiences for which she was only peripherally "present." This compartmentalizing is called *disassociation*; in its extreme form it becomes depersonalization or even Multiple Personality Syndrome. This helps to explain the amnesia. It's hard to remember something that you experienced as occurring to someone else.

"Startle response" is an overreaction to a perceived threat. It can manifest itself in an exaggerated physical reaction or shirking away from touch.

If your partner exhibits "startle response" if you touch her, or splits off during physical or emotional contact, it's hard not to feel rejected or personally responsible. Especially during sex, it can be powerfully disconcerting if your partner hits a trigger and begins to get some memory recall. If she's unable to verbalize what's going on, you will probably feel shut out or like you did something wrong. You may find yourself either blaming her for being too sensitive or starting to "walk on eggshells."

You may discover that you've come to monitor your level of emotional, physical, and/or sexual expression to match your partner's, just as when someone whispers, you find yourself whispering in response. This "equilibration" or mimicking is a part of every human relationship because it helps the bonding process. But if you've unconsciously adapted to your partner's wound, you may be feeling emotionally or sexually shut down or cut off. Or you may realize that there are particular areas that have become "off-limits" in your sexual or emotional relating. This happens when you've felt your partner's anxiety level rise if you've stumbled into a repressed memory and learned not to touch that spot.

The way through this phase of confusion and guilt is *communication*. You and your partner have to be able to identify and define what's going on before anything can change.

Breaking Denial

If you don't know if your partner is an incest survivor, the first step is to get educated about the signs and symptoms of sexual abuse. Read through the checklist on pages 12–14 for further information about how to identify unremembered sexual abuse.

If your partner hasn't identified herself as a survivor, you may want to do some gentle questioning. It's useful to examine whether you've got any judgments or negative feelings toward your partner before you enter discussion. Society has blamed women for sexual experiences all the way back to Eve. Examine yourself for any negative thoughts or feelings. If you discover anger, blame, or judgment, take responsibility to direct it anywhere but at your partner. That would be extremely damaging and should be avoided at all costs. You're not responsible for your cultural conditioning or your first reactions but you are responsible for what you do with them. Talk them out with someone who understands or write them out. Once you've cleared yourself of negative reactions as much as possible, experiment with talking to your partner about possible childhood sexual abuse. Open-ended, nonjudgmental questions are best, such as:

"What are your memories about how your family handled sex?"

"Do you have any bad memories about sex?"

"Have you had any negative sexual experiences you can remember?"

"Have you ever wondered if you were abused as a child?" OR

"I've been reading about signs and symptoms of childhood abuse and notice some of these seem to fit you. I'm not trying to label you—only you can do that; but I'm wondering if you'd want to read about it and talk later."

Once your partner has identified herself as as survivor, there are likely to be new levels of emotion to experience.

Anger

Discovering that your partner (or anyone you know) is an incest survivor typically produces shock and then outrage toward the perpetrator. You may have an instinctive protective response and/or revenge fantasies toward the perpetrator or a lot of general anger you don't know what to do with.

Pain

This may be followed by intense sadness and pain for the "little girl" part of your friend. The anger and pain may alternate or you may tend more toward one or the other. It is very important for you to allow yourself to express your feelings in a safe place. Unfortunately, if your partner is dealing with a lot of her own feelings, she may not be able to respond to yours. Consider an Incest Survivor Partners Support group, a men's therapy group (if you are a heterosexual couple), or some individual or couples' counseling. You need to find some tools and people to work through your feelings with.

If your partner uses the discovery of incest to get into recovery, she will go through stages of grief, rage, and needing to learn how to nurture herself. There will probably continue to be limits on emotional, physical, and sexual expression, at least for a period of time. Your partner will need some kind of support for this issue other than the relationship. Incest survivor recovery is a complex process and it's very important for her to connect with other survivors and possibly therapists. This will probably necessitate some periods of pulling away from you. The relationship will need to change. Your partner may be limited in what she can contribute to the relationship when she's working on her own healing.

If she goes through a period where she needs to not be sexual, you will understandably feel loneliness and frustration. You may find yourself getting angry at your partner, feeling ripped off, and then angry at yourself for feeling this way. Male partners often feel responsible and/or apologetic and guilty just for being a man.

At this point, you will need someone to talk to. Get a support system. Learn to express your own feelings and state your needs and wants. Incest Survivors Partners Support groups or men's groups are very useful. Other important groups to know about are:

Co-dependent's Anonymous

Al-Anon

Parents United

See Chapter Two on "Seeking Support" to learn how to contact them.

If your partner decides not to seek external support, there may be limits on the growth potential of the relationship. You need to decide if you can live with those limits or what your options are if she can't meet your needs. Be clear with her and yourself about your choices and then take action on them.

No matter what your partner does, you will need to focus on:

YOUR RECOVERY

Explore yourself.

Take responsibility for the part of yourself that connected with your partner. On an unconscious level, we always pick partners for a reason.

Ask yourself:

What is there for you to learn through this relationship?

Are there any similar issues in your family of origin?

Was there any sexual abuse in your family?

Are there negative sexual experiences in your own history?

Have you ever been the victim or perpetrator of abuse of any kind?

What are your feelings about sex in general and your own sexuality?

Do you have a need to be a caretaker? Is this covering some wounded part of yourself?

Do you know how to keep the focus on yourself and nurture yourself when you're in a relationship without abandoning yourself or your partner?

Remember . . . there is always a reason for everything we attract into our lives.

It is possible to create a healthy sexual relationship at the appropriate time in both of your recoveries. To do this, you will need to learn about boundaries and triggers and work together on issues of trust and healthy separateness. You will need to learn about nurturing yourself.

As is suggested here, recovery involves summoning a lot of courage. It requires walking into a very dark place and "facing the shadow." It means learning how to sit through what feels like unbearable emotion and trusting that there will be an emergence through to the other side. All people who have lived through these experiences become more whole, integrated, loving, and powerful. The "shadow" always bears a gift; usually it is associated with a clearer connection with one's essence or purpose.

Incest recovery may bring a lesson about what is really valuable and meaningful for an individual or couple. It is possible to recover together and use the discovery of incest to move to a deeper level of love.

A Note to Therapists Working with Survivors

One researcher notes that "the feelings arising in the transference [the relationship between therapist and survivor] may be experienced as assaultive or intrusive, and the apparently mature side of the [survivor] may be siding with the therapist to avoid, rather than deal with the trauma." Therefore, "consequences for psychotherapy are that it should progress beyond a surface description to the painful feelings at a lower level." (Krener, 1985.) Lindberg and Distad (1985) suggest the following for treatment implications: Survivors need to: "1) Express their feelings about the experience, 2) realize their participation in the incest was in no way their fault or responsibility, 3) discern the family dynamics in their own individual experiences, 4) understand how incest leads to self-defeating behavior patterns, 5) reduce stress and build self-esteem by learning new adaptive behaviors."

Therapeutic goals mentioned by Geraldine Faria

and Nancy Belonlavek in "Treating Female Adult Survivors of Childhood Incest" (1984) are the following:

The first goal of treatment is . . . to establish a commitment . . . [to] . . . therapy.

The second goal is to identify old patterns by which [the client] flees from relationships. These patterns may surface again, because . . . [survivors] . . . have such a difficult time being vulnerable and trusting someone else, including a therapist. A key component of treatment is to engage . . . immediately in an active role in the therapy process.

Third, the process of developing a mutual working relationship will aid [her] . . . in becoming aware of [her] own internal strengths and skills and enable [her] to regain control while letting go of learned helplessness. Therapy . . . cannot be complete until [a survivor] is able to trust her therapist and significant other persons and give up the "victim behavior" in order to adopt a self-management approach to . . . life.

The fourth goal is to build . . . self-esteem about survival. This is done by: 1) assuring the survivor that she's a valuable person and has strength, which is evident in the fact that she has survived until this point; 2) alleviating shame about her experience; and 3) accepting and supporting the survivor's intense feelings, especially her anger.

The fifth goal is the constructive expression of anger. . . . It has been the author's experience that victims fall somewhere between either being unable to externalize their anger (thereby becoming more suicidal and self-mutilating), or inappropriately dumping their anger. Dumping often takes the form of verbal and physical abuse, often inflicted on individuals closest to them. Anger and rage require immediate attention. (Having a therapist who can [s]et limits and offer suggestions for the appropriate handling of anger during therapy sessions give[s a survivor] permission to express anger in a safe environment. It allows her to test alternative methods of emotional expression. . . .)

The sixth goal is to identify and gain control over self-destructive and self-defeating behavior such as suicide attempts, self-mutilation, and substance abuse.

I would place the sixth goal as a first priority. What this means in terms of treatment is that the therapist must use careful assessment in timing interpretations and interventions with incest material that is still repressed. However, as Lindberg and Distad write:

Therapists must be aggressive in their history-taking, realizing that the onset of emotional problems in some adults may be a long-term stress reaction to a hidden incest trauma. Interventions need to be centered on trust acquired through reassurance and long-term commitment to the client. Public reaction to incest is so negative that these women sometimes believe that if their incest was discovered they'd be considered worthless, deviant, or tainted. A therapist needs to communicate he/she does not share this attitude so that the client can become less defensive and begin to disclose the details of their past traumas.

Remembering painful events can be a difficult task because survivors have become so accustomed to using repression and denial for emotional survival. There may be enormous anxiety as feelings concerning the traumatic events begin to thaw. Victims have spent years masking their rage, sadness and ambivalence toward the family that betrayed them. The therapy must allow the pain and anger to surface. The severity of the survivors' guilt and shame requires frequent reassurance. They often feel deep self-hatred and disgust that: they couldn't say no, remove themselves from the situation, and/or that they felt aroused and pleasure during parts of the molest.

Bibliography

Armstrong, Louise. *Kiss Daddy Goodnight: A Speak Out on Incest.* New York: Hawthone Press, 1978.

Bass, Ellen, and Laura Davis. *Courage to Heal.* New York: Harper & Row, 1988.

Bass, Ellen. *I Never Told Anyone.* New York: Harper & Row, 1983.

Black, Claudia. *It Will Never Happen to Me.* Denver: M.A.C., 1981.

Boston Women's Health Collective. *The New Our Bodies, Ourselves.* New York: Simon & Schuster, 1984.

Brown, Stephanie. *A Developmental Model of Recovery.* New York: John Wiley & Sons, 1985.

Butler, Sandra. *Conspiracy of Silence: The Trauma of Incest.* San Francisco: New Glide Publications, 1978.

Chandler, Mitzi. *Whiskey's Song.* Pompano Beach, Fla: Health Communications, 1987.

Colgrove, Melba, Harold Bloomfield, and Peter Mc-

Williams. *How to Survive the Loss of a Love*. New York: Bantam Books, 1976.

Courtois, Christine. *Healing the Incest Wound: Adult Survivors in Therapy*. New York: W. W. Norton & Company, 1988.

Diagnostic and Statistical Manual of Mental Disorders, 3rd ed., rev. Washington, D.C.: American Psychiatric Association, 1987.

Ellenson, Gerald. "Disturbances of Perception in Adult Female Incest Survivors," *Social Casework: The Journal of Contemporary Social Work* (March 1986).

Faria, Geraldine, and Nancy Belonlavek. "Treating Female Adult Survivors of Childhood Incest," *Social Casework* 64 (October 1984): 465–71.

Forward, Susan, and Craig Buck. *Betrayal of Innocence: Incest and Its Devastation*. Los Angeles: J. B. Tarcher, 1978.

Fox, Emmett. *Sermon on the Mount*. San Francisco: Harper & Row, 1938.

Fraser, Sylvia. *My Father's House, A Memoir of Incest and Healing*. New York: Harper & Row, 1987.

Friday, Nancy. *My Secret Garden*. New York: Pocket Books, 1973.

Gawain, Shakti, and Laurel King. *Living in the Light*. Mill Valley, Ca.: Whatever Publishing, 1986.

Gawain, Shakti. *Creative Visualization*. New York: Bantam Books, 1978.

Gelinas, Denise. "The Persisting Negative Effects of Incest," *Psychiatry* 46 (November 1983).

Gill, Eliana. *Outgrowing the Pain*. San Francisco: Launch Press, 1984.

Holmes, Ernest. *The Science of Mind*. New York: Dodd, 1989.

Jampolski, Gerald. *Love Is Letting Go of Fear.* New York: Bantam Books, 1970.

Krener. "After Incest, Secondary Prevention?" *Journal of American Academy of Child Psychiatry* 24, 7 (1985): 231–34.

Larsen, Earnie. *Stage II Recovery.* San Francisco: Harper & Row, 1985.

Larsen, Earnie. *Stage II Relationships.* San Francisco: Harper & Row, 1987.

Lindberg, F., and Lois Distad. "Post Traumatic Stress Disorders in Women Who Experienced Childhood Incest," *Child Abuse and Neglect* 9 (1985): 329–34.

Loulan, Joann. *Lesbian Passion—Loving Ourselves and Each Other.* San Francisco: Spinsters/Aunt Lute, 1987.

Maltz, Wendy, and Beverly Holman. *Incest and Sexuality: A Guide to Understanding and Healing.* Lexington, Mass.: Lexington Books, 1987.

Maslow, Abraham. *Toward a Psychology of Being.* New York: Van Nos Reinhold, 1968.

Mason, Jerry. *The Family of Women.* New York: Gross & Dunlap, 1979.

Meiselman, Karin. *Incest: A Psychological Study of Causes and Effects with Treatment Recommendations.* San Francisco: Jossey-Bass, 1979.

Owens, Travis. "Personality Traits of Female Psychotherapy Patients with a History of Incest: A Research Note." *Journal of Personality Assessments* Vol 48, 6 (1984): 606–08.

Peck, M. Scott. *The Road Less Traveled.* New York: Simon & Schuster, 1978.

Ponder, Catherine. *Dynamic Laws of Prosperity.* Englewood Hills, N.J.: Prentice Hall, 1962.

Poston, Carol, and Karen Lison. *Reclaiming Our Lives: Adult Survivors of Incest.* Boston: Little, Brown, 1989.

Ray, Sondra. *I Deserve Love.* Millbrae, Calif.: Les Femmes Publishing, 1976.

Ray, Sondra. *The Only Diet There Is.* Berkeley, Calif.: Celestial Arts, 1981.

Rosenberg, Jack. *Body, Self and Soul: Sustaining Integration.* Atlanta, Ga.: Humanics, 1985.

Ross, Ruth. *Prospering Woman.* Mill Valley: Whatever Publishing, 1982.

Roth, Geneen. *Feeding the Hungry Heart.* New York: Signet Books, 1982.

Russell, Diana. *The Secret Trauma.* New York: Basic Books, 1986.

Tower, Cynthia. *Secret Scars.* New York: Penguin Books, 1988.

Utain, Marsha, and Barbara Oliver. *Scream Louder.* Deerfield Beach, Fla.: Health Communications, 1989.

Vander Mey, Brenda, and Ronald Neff. "Adult-Child Incest: A Review of Research and Treatment." *Adolescence* XVII, 68 (1982): 717–33.

Vander Mey, Brenda, and Ronald Neff. "Adult-Child Incest: A Sample of Substantiated Cases." *Family Relations* 33 (1984).

Whitfield, Charles. *Healing the Child Within.* Deerfield Beach, Fla.: Health Communications, 1989.

Winston, Stephanie. *Getting Organized.* New York: Warner Books, 1979.

Wood, Wendy, and Leslie Hutton. *Triumph over Darkness.* Hillsboro, Oregon: Beyond Words Publishing, 1989.

By the year 2000, 2 out of 3 Americans could be illiterate.

It's true.

Today, 75 million adults... about one American in three, can't read adequately. And by the year 2000, U.S. News & World Report envisions an America with a literacy rate of only 30%.

Before that America comes to be, you can stop it... by joining the fight against illiteracy today.

Call the Coalition for Literacy at toll-free **1-800-228-8813** and volunteer.

Volunteer Against Illiteracy. The only degree you need is a degree of caring.

Ad Council Coalition for Literacy